Tallaght, 1835–50: a rural place

Maynooth Studies in Local History

SERIES EDITOR   Raymond Gillespie

This volume is one of six short books published in the Maynooth Studies in Local History series in 2008. Like their predecessors most are drawn from theses presented as part of the MA course in local history at NUI Maynooth. Also like their predecessors they range widely over the local experience in the Irish past from the middle ages into the twentieth century. That local experience is presented in the complex social world of which it is part. These were diverse worlds that need to embrace such differing experiences as the fisheries of Arklow, or the world of books and reading in Loughrea. For yet others their world was constructed through the tensions which resulted in the murder of Major Denis Mahon near Strokestown in 1847. The local experience cannot be a simple chronicling of events relating to an area within administrative or geographically-determined boundaries since understanding the local world presents much more complex challenges for the historian. It is a reconstruction of the socially diverse worlds of poor and rich, from the poor of pre-Famine Tallaght to the more prosperous world of the Church of Ireland in the diocese of Lismore. Reconstructing such diverse local worlds relies on understanding what the people of the different communities that made up the localities of Ireland had in common and what drove them apart. Understanding the assumptions, often unspoken, around which these local societies operated is the key to recreating the world of the Irish past and reconstructing the way in which those who inhabited those worlds lived their daily lives. As such studies like those presented in these short books, together with their predecessors, are at the forefront of Irish historical research and represent some of the most innovative and exciting work being undertaken in Irish history today. They also provide models which others can follow up and adapt in their own studies of the Irish past. In such ways will we understand better the regional diversity of Ireland and the social and cultural basis for that diversity. If they also convey something of the vibrancy and excitement of the world of Irish local history today they will have achieved at least some of their purpose.

Maynooth Studies in Local History: Number 76

Tallaght, 1835–50:
a rural place

Sean Bagnall

FOUR COURTS PRESS

Set in 10pt on 12pt Bembo by
Carrigboy Typesetting Services for
FOUR COURTS PRESS LTD
7 Malpas Street, Dublin 8, Ireland
e-mail: info@fourcourtspress.ie
http://www.fourcourtspress.ie
and in North America for
FOUR COURTS PRESS
c/o ISBS, 920 N.E. 58th Avenue, Suite 300, Portland, OR 97213.

ISBN 978-1-84682-113-4

Printed in England by
Athenaeum Press Ltd, Gateshead, Tyne & Wear.

Contents

Acknowledgments

It is impossible to complete a project such as this without becoming indebted to the many people who in so many ways become involved in its completion. My thanks to Professor Raymond Gillespie, the series editor, for his help and support, both in deciding to include my short book in the Maynooth local history series, and in the editing process where his work and comments did so much to make the study presentable. My thanks also to Professor Vincent Comerford for his infinite patience and guidance in preparing the first draft of this work. At the beginning of my research I was greatly helped by Pat Scanlon at the Valuation Office and his assistance in making available copies of the relevant valuation field books provided much of the material used. The staff at the library in NUI Maynooth were also helpful during the many hours spent researching the parliamentary papers. Thanks also to the staff at the library of the Representative Church Body and at the National Archives of Ireland.

A number of individuals were especially helpful and Kieran Swords at Tallaght library gave me access to the Tallaght library local history collection. Many thanks to my classmates in Maynooth who always supported and encouraged me; their mutual cooperation is a source of sustenance to us all. Dr Frank Sweeney has been especially helpful.

Various members of my own family have provided support over the years not least because of their interest in the history of Tallaght and their connection with it. My wife Maureen and Mercedes, Ken, Jennifer and John have all kept my feet on the ground and I hope they derive some pleasure from this book. The credit is all theirs and the mistakes are my own.

Introduction

In 1837 when Samuel Lewis published his *Topographical dictionary of Ireland* he included a long entry on the parish of Tallaght, Co. Dublin. This celebrated a number of aspects of the place. It recorded its remarkable medieval history, its ecclesiastical state and, most prominently, the seats of the gentry living there. It described Belgard Castle, the seat of P.H. Cruise, and named some 27 other 'remarkable seats'. This study deals with another Tallaght. It is not, in the main, concerned with the gentry, but with the ordinary people of Tallaght in the period 1835 to 1851 and especially the poor, who are usually omitted from such stories, in the period before the Great Famine. Central to this is the physical world of Tallaght and its people at about 1835, which can be reconstructed using parliamentary papers together with the Griffith Valuation and the valuation field books. These sources tell us a great deal about how the people lived, what life was like for the people of Tallaght and what may have happened to those people during the period up to 1851.

The civil parish of Tallaght was an extensive and varied place. It stretched from the present village of Templeogue to the top of Glenasmole and bordered Co. Wicklow at Kippure, Seefingan and Corrig Mountains and also met the Kildare boundary at Brittas. It comprised 21,867 acres in 49 separate townlands.[1] North of Oldbawn the land lies at or below 100 metres above sea level. South of that it rises steadily until it reaches 757 metres at the top of Kippure, the highest point in Co. Dublin.[2] Land quality varied from the very good lands of Ballyroan and Tymon South to the moorlands on the slopes of Kippure Mountain.

In 1821 the census of that year recorded 4,348 people in the parish of Tallaght. The population of Tallaght for that and the following years are set out together with an index of the population increases and decreases for the period (taking 1821 as the base year) in table 1 on page 9.

From 1841 onwards the census returns also give information about the population of each townland in the parish and so an examination can be made of the way people moved about and were distributed in the parish from that date onwards. The returns also give information on literacy levels, religious profession, mortality, age, occupations and causes of death.

Other material from among the parliamentary papers, church records, outrage papers and a small number of books written on the subject allow a reconstruction to be made of the world of mid nineteenth-century Tallaght

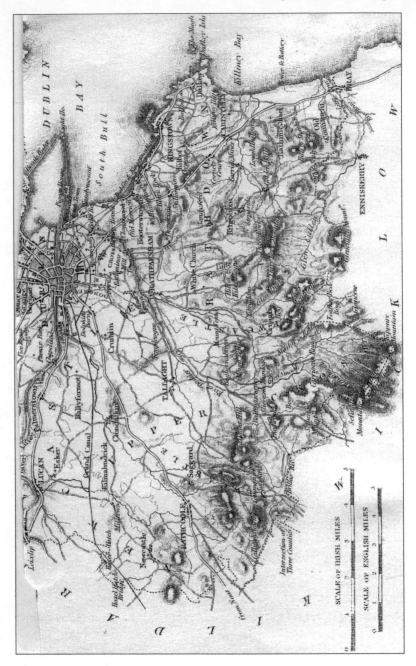

1. Tallaght in the context of Co. Dublin, 1837

Table 1 Index of population changes

Year	Population	Index of Population changes
1821	4,348	100
1831	4,646	107
1841	4,921	113
1851	4,367	100
1861	3,831	88
1871	3,584	82

Source: *Abstract of the answers and returns, pursuant to act 55 Geo. 3, for taking an account of the population of Ireland in 1821, H.C. 1824 (577), xxii, p. 18* (hereinafter cited as *Census, Ireland, 1821.*) *Abstract of answers and returns under the population acts Ireland: enumeration 1831, H.C. 1833, (634), xxxix p. 22* (hereinafter cited as *Census, Ireland, 1831.*) *Report of the commissioners appointed to take the census of Ireland for the year 1841, H.C. 1843, [504], xxiv, p. 30* (hereinafter cited as *Census, Ireland, 1841.*) *Report of the commissioners appointed to take the census of Ireland for the year 1851, H.C. 1852–3, p. 42* (hereinafter cited as *Census, Ireland, 1851.*) *The census of Ireland for 1861, H.C. 1863, vol i p. 42.* (hereinafter cited as *Census, Ireland, 1861.*)

including its physical world and the struggle for survival of the people who inhabited that world. This same area returned a population of 4,565 persons in the census for 1961 indicating a long period of relatively little change. The presence of many family names at the same locations from the early nineteenth century until the mid twentieth century also supports this. But the scale of change in Tallaght since 1970 means there are now very few inhabitants with memories or knowledge of that earlier world. This book may rectify a small part of that deficit.

Index number	Townland name	Area in acres	1850 Valuation Land only	1850 Valuation per acre IR£
1	Aughfarrell	581.68	166.85	0.29
2	Allagour	83	50.55	0.61
3	Ballinascorney lower	177.29	142.65	0.80
4	Ballinascorney Upper	2275.8	367.4	0.16
5	Ballycragh	102.58	210.6	2.05
6	Ballycullen	112.23	201.45	1.79
7	Ballymaice	170.67	123.45	0.72
8	Ballymana	444.56	282.75	0.64
9	Ballymorefinn	532.24	97.45	0.18
10	ballyroan	114.29	259.15	2.27
11	Belgard	323.06	450.25	1.39
12	Belgard Deerpark	123.97	49.65	0.40
13	Bohernabreena	231.74	297.15	1.28
14	Brittas Big	140.27	132.3	0.94
15	Brittas Little	250.71	149.15	0.59
16	Castlekelly	2797.38	104.1	0.04
17	Cookstown	264.64	422.75	1.60
18	Corbally	523.86	368.2	0.70
19	Corrageen	21.71	13.65	0.63
20	Cunard	257.3	42.85	0.17
21	Friarstown Lower	54.04	34.9	0.65
22	Friarstown Upper	179.35	146.3	0.82
23	Garranstown or Kingswood	122.76	220.85	1.80
24	Gibbons	247.88	255.5	1.03
25	Glassamucky	422	219.05	0.52
26	Glassamucky Brakes	1115.63	131.75	0.12
27	Glassamucky Mountain	176.03	2.25	0.01
28	Glassavullaun	1090.62	78.05	0.07
29	Gortlum	342.4	220.4	0.64
30	Jobstown	420.52	448.4	1.07
31	Killinarden	515.32	393.35	0.76
32	Killininny	194.57	314.6	1.62
33	Kilnamanagh	621.63	1342.4	2.16
34	Kiltalown	277.24	259.85	0.94
35	Kiltipper	193.12	180.5	0.93
36	Knocklyon	429.71	989.45	2.30
37	Lugmore	122.45	53	0.43
38	Mountpelier	919.83	318.9	0.35
39	Mountseskin	715.73	285	0.40
40	Newlands Demesne	70.32	131.4	1.87
41	Oldbawn	615.31	805	1.31
42	Oldcourt	435.89	642.95	1.48
43	Piperstown	381.05	97.85	0.26
44	Tallaght	1052.47	1786.9	1.70
45	Templeogue	671.13	1381.9	2.06
46	Tymon North	483.41	891.2	1.84
47	Tymon South	105.26	250.6	2.38
48	Whitehall	122.68	146.25	1.19
49	Whitestown	240.97	293.45	1.22
		21,868.30	16,254.35	0.74

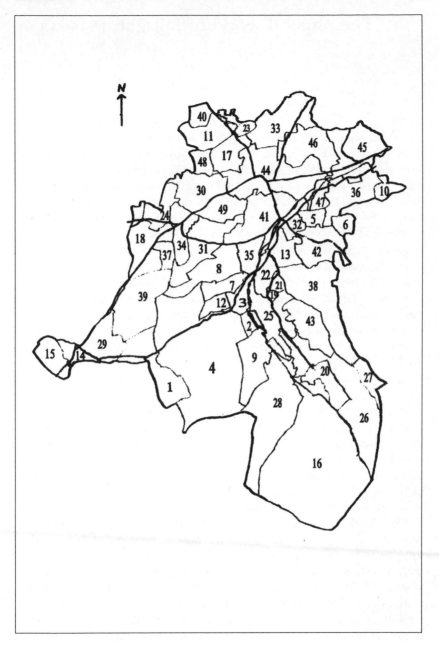

2. Townland index map

1. The physical world of Tallaght, 1835–44

The original village of Tallaght is located approximately 13 kilometres south-west of the centre of Dublin and is bisected by the N81 road from Dublin to Blessington. Until about 1969 this was a rural village surrounded by farmland. But since then major urban development has transformed Tallaght into a substantial town of over 120,000 people in less than 40 years. It is now the administrative centre of the South Dublin County Council and a major centre of industry, shopping and health care.

This study is concerned with the old civil parish of Tallaght and in broad terms this extended along the Dodder valley from Templeogue village to the top of Kippure Mountain on the Dublin–Wicklow border as outlined in figure 2. There is a natural division in this parish where the Dodder River leaves the valley of Glenasmole at Bohernabreena. North and north-east of this the land was rich and flat, of good quality and well drained. It is now almost totally developed as residential housing and slopes gently from an elevation of *c.*120m above sea level at Bohernabreena to *c.*50m at Templeogue. To the east this part of the parish is bounded by the townlands of Orlagh, Woodtown, Ballyboden and the divided townland of Ballyroan. To the west Clondalkin and Saggart bound the parish. South of Bohernabreena the land rises from the floor of the glacial valley of Glenasmole to the heights of Mountpelier, Piperstown and Glassamucky Mountain on the east side and Ballinascorney, Ballymorefinn, Glassavullaun and Castlekelly to the west with Kippure Mountain at the head of the valley. Here the land reaches a height of 757m above sea level, thus rising over 630m in the approximately 9km trek from Bohernabreena. This part of the parish borders on county Wicklow and further west, at Brittas, the parish touches Co. Kildare.[1]

The River Dodder rises in several streams on the northern slopes of Kippure and forms a single river on the floor of Glenasmole. It leaves this valley at Bohernabreena and flows north-easterly towards Templeogue. It is the main watercourse in the parish and in the past it provided water power to several mills along its length. There were several main roads through the parish. The most important of these was the main road from Dublin through Crumlin, Greenhills and Kilnamanagh to Tallaght Village and on through Brittas to Blessington. This was the main road to Carlow and for a time functioned as the Carlow Turnpike. Another important road was that from Rathfarnham to Ballinascorney. This road passed through Firhouse, Kilininney and Bohernabreena before rising to Ballinascorney. These roads were crossed by the road from Orlagh to Clondalkin. This route passed through Old Court, Kilininney, Old Bawn, Tallaght and Cookstown before coming to Clondalkin. It crossed the Rathfarnham to Ballinascorney road at Kilininney; the Dodder at Old Bawn and the Carlow Turnpike in Tallaght Village. A further road passed through Terenure and Templeogue before joining the Carlow Turnpike in Tallaght. These roads are shown on the map in figure 2.

Griffith's Valuation, carried out in this parish in 1844, recorded the varying land quality within the parish. The best quality land was on the lower lands to the north and north-east of the parish. This land had an average valuation in excess of £1 per acre. Where the land starts to rise towards the mountains land quality deteriorated and this poorer land had an average valuation of between 10s. and £1. Land of this quality runs from the Glenasmole Valley in a westerly loop towards the parish of Saggart and occurs again at Brittas. The poorest land in the parish in 1844 was found on all the uplands ranging to the top of Kippure and forming a horseshoe around Glenasmole. Thus the parish of Tallaght had land quality varying from the very best of farmland on the edge of the city to high, wild and desolate moorlands in the mountains at the Wicklow border.

POPULATION AND ITS GEOGRAPHY IN TALLAGHT

The population of Tallaght can be estimated from both Griffith's Valuation and the census returns for the years 1821 to 1871. No information is available giving population figures by townland until the census of 1841, so before that year it is not possible to examine the dispersal of the population in the parish. From this census data the townland size, population and average household size for each townland have been calculated in the appendix. This appendix also shows the number of occupied houses per townland as counted by the Griffith valuators in the field books in 1844 and in the Valuation of Tenements completed in 1850.

The population of the parish of Tallaght in 1841 was 4,921 persons. The average population density was 0.23 persons per acre in 1841 but this varied from over one person per acre in Corrageen and Tymon South to the emptiness of Belgard Deerpark and Glassamucky Mountain. By 1851 the average population density had fallen to 0.20 people per acre in the parish. Friarstown Lower was now the only townland to have a density greater than one person per acre. A statistical analysis of this information indicates that the standard deviation also fell during the 10 year period from 0.22 in 1841 to 0.18 in 1851, indicating that population density levelled out over the parish in the period. The parish had several clusters of population in 1841, defined as groupings of more than 100 people living at densities of greater than a person per two acres. These were at Tallaght village, Tymon South (Firhouse Village), Greenhills (Kilnamanagh), Templeogue, Oldbawn and Knocklyon. Oldbawn is marginal in terms of density. There were also significant densities of people in Allagour, Ballymaice, Corrageen and Friarstown Lower. Ballymaice was the location of a school and the other townlands are notable for being the three smallest townlands in the parish. In all other townlands in the parish the population density was less than one person per 2.5 acres, and in most cases, substantially less. The significant clusters of population were all located in the lowland part of the parish, and the other areas of high density were located on the moderate lands. The poorest uplands all had low population densities. But the highest quality lands did not always have dense populations. An anomaly is presented in the townland of Ballycragh, which had 102 acres of the highest quality land, but had a population of two people in 1841. By 1851 this townland had no population and no dwelling house.

Perhaps the most visible features on the landscape of Tallaght were the mills powered by the Dodder and other streams running off the surrounding hills. Lewis in 1837 commented 'there are several woollen mills and a paper mill in the parish'.[2] The valuation field books[3] give details of these mills in the townlands of Tallaght, Templeogue and Oldbawn. These are set out in table 2. The mills in the townland of Oldbawn were powered by a millrace taken from the Dodder at a point above Kiltipper House between the townlands of Kiltipper and Friarstown Upper. This millrace crossed under the Kiltipper Road just above the house known as Glenville and from there it ran through the fields until it came to McDonnell's paper mill, adjacent to Oldbawn House. The millrace then followed the top of the low ridge of land between Oldbawn and Tallaght running under the Oldbawn Road at the entrance to Samuel Neill's mills. Here it supplied both Neill's Woollen Cloth Mill[4] and McCracken's Flour Mill before turning southeast towards the Dodder. Finally it supplied power to Neill's Flour Mill just before returning to the river.

Michael McDonnell's paper mill was described in the valuation field book as having

> one set of calendars, 5 rag engines, one pump, a devil, all equal to 30 horse power; waterwheel metal 'a', diameter 24 feet; buckets 12 feet; shrouding 14 inches fall 21.9. Column of water 11 feet and 3 inches revolving three and a half times in a minute – making machine equal to 6 horse power; wheel 'b' 13 feet diameter 3 feet buckets. Shrouding 8 inches, fall 11 feet.

Griffith had issued specific instructions as to how these structures were to be valued. In the case of paper mills, saw mills and other general mills the

Table 2 The mills of Oldbawn, Tallaght and Templeogue in 1850

Map reference	Occupier	Description of tenement	Rateable valuation of buildings
Oldbawn			
3a	Samuel Neill Esq	House, offices, weaving factory, flour mill and land	£90
4a	Michael McDonnell Esq	House, offices, papermill and land	£108
8	John McCracken Esq	House, offices, mills and land	£65 14s.
Tallaght			
18a	James Williamson	House, offices, papermill and land	£47 14s.
43	Michael Mahon	Cornmill, offices and land	£5 08s.
Templeogue			
1a	James Sharp	House, offices, flour mill and land	£68 08s.
20Aab	Francis Burke	House, mill, offices and land	£44 02s.
28a	Joseph McDonnell Esq	House, offices, papermill and land	£95 08s.

Source: Griffith, valuation of tenements, 1850

valuers were to assess the actual power supply by an examination of the nature and size of the water wheels together with an examination of the water supply to the wheel pit in both volume and constancy of flow.[5] At £108 valuation McDonnell's mill clearly had a substantial capacity for paper production and, indeed, was the largest in the Tallaght area. The main machine room at McDonnell's mill was described as being 83 ft by 48 ft by 22 ft high and there was an extensive range of ancillary buildings included in this enterprise.

There is other evidence available as to the scale of this manufactory. John D'Alton's *The history of the county of Dublin*[6] was published in 1838 and was probably written not long before that. It stated that this mill employed about 50 persons. There is a contemporary or near contemporary manuscript note in page 757 of the copy in the author's possession amending this to 150 persons. The expansion of the population in the townland of Oldbawn between 1850 and 1851, indicated in the appendix, provides additional evidence for an expansion of employment at this mill during that period. There is a further note in the valuation field book, which was added at some point between the initial valuation survey in 1844 and publication of the Tenement Valuation in 1850, which supports this view. It reads; 'These notes agree with surveyors notes who found new buildings amounting to £22 not erected when this measurement was made. Adopt surveyor's measurement.'7 An expansion of facilities and employment at this mill about 1850 was therefore possible. A further description of this mill was given by H.G. Leask in 1913. He described Oldbawn House, part of which had been given over to paper making. A ground floor room was said to have been used for paper drying and it appears that the paper mill was located adjacent to the house. Leask commented that 'the house suffered from the proximity of the factory, and was in part given over to mill purposes.'8

Conditions in the mills are recorded in the Poor Inquiry of 1835. A master paper manufacturer from the Dublin area reported on that trade as follows:

In 1828 I put up some machinery on my premises about three miles from Dublin, which was set on fire, I suppose, from the workmen thinking some of them would be thrown out of employ. I offered a reward of £100 for the apprehension of the offenders, but it was of no avail. From the machinery being so much more general in England and Scotland an immense quantity of paper is imported here. The duty is 3d in the pound here as well as in England; in consequence of its being so very heavy, many manufacturers have been induced to smuggle, and when discovered, from being compelled to pay the excessive penalties have become ruined.

From want of capital to raise machinery here, the same steamers which bring in goods ready prepared take back our raw materials.

We have often petitioned for the removal, or a reduction of the excise duty, but without effect. We only want protection given to the fair trader.

The workmen are so poor, and our trade so very bad, that I do not think there is any combination amongst them now.

I do not imagine they could make any objection now to the putting up of machinery.

Half the men who used to be employed are now quite idle. Many are gone to America and elsewhere. I pay one-fifth of the whole duty of the County of Dublin. At one period of my life, I have done only half the business I now do, and made double the profit. Every description of trade in Dublin has declined beyond all belief.

Buildings on the quay would not produce anything like half what they would have done a few years since. For the last thirty or forty years there has not been a single person in the paper trade who has not failed but myself; and I think within the last thirty years seven out of ten in every trade in Dublin have failed. For the last ten years I have never reduced the wages of my men. The proportion of the men since I put up the machinery is about one to five.

The full wages are £1 02s. or £1 03s. weekly (€1.40 or €1.46), out of which is deducted 1s for rent. I employ a great number of women and children, and have never had any objection to them.[9]

The report does not identify the paper maker but McDonnell at Oldbawn operated in the same area and market as this man and conditions for McDonnell's millworkers were probably similar. Those who gave the evidence on combinations in the Dublin paper manufacturing trade are not named but some of the comments made indicate a substantial manufacturer accounting for one fifth of the total duty on paper for Co. Dublin. The evidence also stated that the informant charged 1s. per week rent. This statement coincides with the note in the field book to the effect that McDonnell had a tenement at 1s. per week and hence this description may be of McDonnell's mill. Further information about this paper mill indicates further growth before its eventual closing towards the end of the nineteenth century. William Domville Handcock's *History and antiquities of Tallaght* was first published in 1876 and contains a contemporary description of these mills, which were then still managed by a Mr McDonnell. At this stage, in addition to the water wheel, there was one steam engine of 200-horse power and several smaller ones. The second edition of Handcock's book was published in 1899 and notes that this mill had closed in the interim period because the company was unable to compete with foreign manufacture.[10]

Having provided the power for McDonnell's Mill the millrace then passed across the Oldbawn Road to provide power to the mills of Samuel Neill and John McCracken. Neill operated a woollen mill and McCracken a flour mill which were smaller than McDonnell's mill with valuations of £90 and £65 14s. respectively, but still substantial mills by local standards These mills were located almost side-by-side at a place named 'Haarlem' in Oldbawn townland. The millrace then returned to the river and finally provided power to a flour mill belonging to Samuel Neill at the bank of the river. It is possible that the two mills belonging to Samuel Neill were combined at one entry in the printed Griffith's Valuation listing. They were, however, described separately in the field books and shown separately on the valuation maps. Neill's Woollen mill (so described on the valuation map) was described as a tuck mill in the field book. It had '4 stocks – about 35 yards of cloth in each stock every day – water same as in flour mill'.[11]

There was no report in the Poor Inquiry of conditions specifically on the operations in tuck mills but the reports on the woollen manufacturing trade gave some information on conditions in cloth manufacturing generally.

Reports on combinations in the woollen manufacture trade indicated a degree of friction between mill owners and workers in this trade.[12] One person giving evidence to the Poor Inquiry in 1834 reported that in 1811 men were paid 28s. weekly and now they are paid 16s.; women and children are now paid the same as in 1811. The same person said that foremen's wages had not changed over the same period.[13] Another reported that: 'Twenty years before the Union fine cloth was made here [in Dublin] in considerable quantities; but from the improvements in machinery and skill in England, we were soon undersold in this market'.

It was also reported that

> In 1814 factories for stuff, on the new system of machinery, first commenced. Two children will now do as much in spinning as 100 women could do by hand … the stuff weavers do not now earn more than 5s. a week, working from five in the morning till ten at night … An individual at Celbridge is now erecting a power loom for weaving, by which means a girl will be able to do as much work as six men, and will thus entirely destroy the trade of one of the witnesses. The individual in question will be able to get as much work done for 2s. as would cost the witness 18s. For the best flannel the witness makes he gets a shilling and a farthing a yard (the latter is all his profit); and the retail shopkeeper to whom he sells it, often gets as much as 5d per yard profit on it.[14]

D'Alton recorded that Neill's woollen factory gave employment to about 70 people and it described its site as 'formerly the most celebrated bleach green in Ireland.'[15] He also reported the setting up of a trust in 1812 to be applied for the relief of the poor of Haarlem where the mills were located. This indicates a community close to and probably dependant on the mills and a degree of poverty among them at that stage. The woollen mill at Oldbawn existed at a time of considerable change in the Irish textile manufacturing trade generally. The major weaving and spinning towns in England were growing and, with changing technology, were expanding output of mass produced cloth, both woollen and cotton. This inevitably had an impact on the Irish trade as new technology was adopted there and there is no reason to believe that people in Oldbawn were any different to those elsewhere.

John McCracken's flour mill was alongside Neill's woollen factory and it seems to have been a substantial enterprise with three pairs of mill stones. The Valuation field book entry also described the capacity of the mill as 'employing 7 months and 22 hours in the day and 5 months and 6 hours in the day'. The usual description of the waterwheel is then given. The valuers instructions tabled the system by which flour mills were to be rated.[16]

Numbers of millstones were one factor, hours worked was another and 22 hours in the day was regarded as a full time mill. Thereafter distance from a major population centre was taken into account, as was any fluctuation in water supply. Neill's flour mill, located close to the Dodder, was employed 20 hours a day for six months of the year and six hours a day for the remainder of the year. The mill wheels were described as two pairs of French burrs each four feet four inches in diameter. There followed a description of the waterwheel. The mill itself measured 56 feet by 44 feet by 28 feet high. It was a considerable structure. The field book also has a note written across this entry: 'This mill was burned lately and not as yet rebuilt–July 1847'. However it was rated and included in the list of Valuation of Tenements published in 1850, suggesting that it was subsequently rebuilt. No trace remains of the weir which diverted portion of the Dodder into the millrace for the Oldbawn mills. Handcock described this weir as being built of loose stone and sods of earth. He stated that it was susceptible to being swept away by floods and that when such events happened the mills described stood idle until the weir was repaired.[17]

There were two mills in the townland of Tallaght. The first of these was a small corn mill occupied by Michael Mahon. There is no entry for this mill in the section of the field books giving details of the larger mills and houses. The mill was located close to Tallaght Village and utilised the stream which eventually joined the Dodder River close to Firhouse (Tymon South). Its valuation of £5 8s. suggests a very small enterprise. Griffith set a table as a 'ready reckoner' for assessing the valuation of waterpower to drive a pair of millstones on which the lowest rating was £6 for the lowest quality of machinery working for 8 hours per day[18] and these may be the conditions in the mill just described since the valuation was so close to £6. This mill was assessed at a lower figure than this. Handcock referred to an old Manor Mill located just below the town of Tallaght.[19] In the Ordnance Survey Letters there is reference to a very small old mill in a letter from Eugene O'Curry to Thomas Larcom dated 17 August 1837. It was located just outside Tallaght Village on the Oldbawn road and was described as being the 'smallest and the oldest mill that I have ever seen'. There are two pairs of stones set going by an over shot power and capable of grinding about 4 barrels of wheat in 24 hours'.[20] John Newcomen's map of Tallaght drawn in 1654 did include two buildings adjacent to the watercourse at Tallaght but neither of these was described as a mill.[21] However, these buildings were both in the approximate position of the mill as shown in the 1831 Ordnance Survey map, adjacent to the stream opposite the road which came to Tallaght from Greenhills.

The other mill in Tallaght was a paper mill located at 'Bolbrook', between the Templeogue road and the river just as the river reached Firhouse. It seems to have been a less extensive enterprise than the McDonnell's mill at Oldbawn with a valuation of only £47 in 1850. The main mill building measured 78ft by 22ft and 17ft high. It was described as having a 'bad loft'. An extensive range of stores, offices and drying lofts surrounded it. The water was employed 12 hours a day for eight months in the year and 9 hours a day for the rest of the year.[22]

Three mills were included in the Valuation list for Templeogue in 1850 powered by the very old millrace taken from the Dodder at the Firhouse weir. This millrace is reported to have been built in the 13th century, not as a millrace, but to supply water to Dublin.[23] The weir in Firhouse, from which this watercourse starts was a far more substantial affair than the weir diverting the Oldbawn millrace. Within a very short distance of the Firhouse weir, this watercourse provided power to Mr Joseph McDonnell's paper mill. These mills, close to the weir and in the townland of Templeogue, were almost as extensive as McDonnell's mills at Oldbawn with the water 'employed day and night for six months of the year and about 1/3 time at work during the other 6 months. Works by waterpower equal to 20 horse power'.[24] Some description of the ancillary buildings was given in the 1844 valuation field books including a rag boiling room, indicating at least some of the raw materials used. Two offices were described as 'Old Saul' and a 'Size House'. Among the mill buildings was a tenement paying 1s. per week rent and the clerk's dwelling was described as measuring 27ft by 17ft and 5ft high.

The next mill on this water course was the flour mill occupied by Francis Burke. It was located close to the present Cheeverstown House. This was not so large as the mill of John McCracken at Oldbawn having just one pair of French Burr millstones measuring 4 feet 8 inches in diameter. North of this location in the Templeogue townland was the flour mill of James Sharpe. This mill could process 3,600 barrels of flour in the year. It had two pairs of French burr millstones but the valuation field book records that they were: 'seldom wrought at the same time but one pair is constantly wrought with dressing machine and screens'. This flour mill measured 36ft by 44ft by 21ft high and was named 'Mount Down Flour Mill' in the Ordnance Survey map for 1831.

Thus the Dodder Valley between Oldbawn and Templeogue hosted one woollen mill, four flour mills, three paper mills and one corn mill in 1844 when the valuation field books were compiled. The valuation lists and accompanying maps indicate that there were substantial clusters of 11 small houses located at the McDonnell paper mill at Oldbawn and another 11 at the group of mills at Haarlem in Oldbawn also. There were other groups of small houses in Oldbawn which were let by a Bridget Reilly and by a Felix J. Woods, amounting to 7 houses and 11 houses respectively. The presence of these houses indicates families of labourers either dependant on the mills or on other employment such as agriculture in the immediate area. The evidence on the state of the woollen trade discussed above indicates that it was usual for women and children to be employed in the mills so the women of the family may have found employment elsewhere, as in agriculture when no work was available in the mills. From the dimension of the mills and their rating it appears that the McDonnells and the Neills had the largest mills and were the biggest employers in the area, employing up to 150 and 70 people respectively. There was a smaller cluster of eight houses at Williamson's mill at Bolbrook in Tallaght. There were no significant groups of houses associated with the mills of Sharpe or Burke. McDonnell at Templeogue had a cluster of 12 small houses around his paper mill which was a substantial enterprise. It was almost as large as that at Oldbawn and it would be reasonable to expect that it employed a similar number of workers. The numbers employed probably fell in the 1840s as there was a reduction in the population of Templeogue from 1841 to 1851 and there is no other evidence that the Templeogue paper mill expanded. The census for 1841 provides further information about employment in the area.[25] In the summary to the general table families were classified according to their pursuits as chiefly employed in one of three forms of employment namely, agriculture, manufactures, or trade. In this, 651 families in Tallaght parish were classified as chiefly employed in agriculture and 123 families were chiefly employed in manufacturing or trade. A further 77 families had other pursuits. Thus the majority of families in the parish (76.5%) were engaged in agriculture and 14.45% were engaged in manufacture. If this ratio of families in Tallaght translated into people, then 14.45% of the 1841 population represented 711 people engaged in or dependant on manufacture or trade in Tallaght in that year. This indicates that Tallaght had a strongly rural character at that time with the overwhelming majority of the population engaged in agriculture. Figures for agricultural production in 1841 are not available but the figures for 1851 give some idea of the types of farming in the parish. But the intervention of the Famine did change farm structure and agricultural output towards a cash economy[26] so that these figures are only indicative of farming output in 1841. They are set out in table 3 on page 22.

These returns are remarkable for the variety of crops grown including extensive acreages of wheat and oats. The contiguous existence of the Dublin market makes it likely that many of these crops were supplied to feed the city before 1845. The total area of the parish was 21,867 acres so that 12.5% of the land area in the parish was under crops in 1851. The remainder of the land produced meadow or clover, or was used as pasture or rough mountain grazing.[27] This agricultural environment accounted for 76.5% of employment in the parish in 1841 and compared with 59% in the whole of Leinster, 71% in Munster, 61% in Ulster and 78% in Connacht. The average percentage so employed in the whole of Ireland was 66%. Thus Tallaght was typically rural and despite its closeness to Dublin City it had employment patterns similar to those in Connacht or Munster rather than Leinster.

Table 3 Crop survey, 1851[28]

Name of crop	Acres	Name of crop	Acres
Wheat	370	Carrots	1
Oats	1,732	Parsnips	2
Barley	63	Cabbage	4
Bere	13	Vetches	22
Rye	2	Other green crops	20
Beans	1	Flax	1
Potatoes	374	Rape	8
Turnips	127		
Mangel	11	Total	2,751

Source: Census, Ireland, 1851, p. 223.

In addition to the mills described above there may have been some limited commercial life in the parish of Tallaght but details are hard to find. The contemporary commercial directories for Dublin dealt with the city only. However, the valuation field books indicated some businesses and some commercial activity in Tallaght, including a number of public houses, forges, a shop and a post office in the parish. There were also several sand and gravel pits. Many of the farms were described as having dairies, gardens or orchards whose produce could be consumed in subsistence living or sold for cash. A study of these commercial establishments indicates that the most numerous enterprises at the time were gravel pits. There were 11 premises described as gravel pits in the valuation field books with an additional two 'old gravel pits'. The use of the word 'old' may indicate that these pits had already fallen into disuse. All of the sand and gravel pits and quarries noted in the valuation field books in 1844–5 are listed in table 4.

Three of the gravel pits were located in Kilnamanagh and the Ordnance Survey map of 1831 indicated a further grouping of gravel pits in the adjacent townland of Greenhills in the parish of Crumlin. They were located in the area between Kilnamanagh and the present Walkinstown junction and were mostly adjacent to the main road from Tallaght to Dublin. The Greenhills road followed the top of an esker ridge of sandhills and the result of the extraction activity is today indicated by the sharp fall from that road to the housing and industrial estates which line it. This grouping of gravel pits was also located in that area of the parish closest to Dublin and their output was probably consumed in the building boom in late 18th and early 19th century in Dublin.[29] The remaining gravel pits were scattered in

Table 4 Survey of gravel pits in 1844–5

Description	Townland	Occupier
Gravel pit	Kilnamanagh	Anne Tracy
Gravel pit	Kilnamanagh	William Allen
Gravel pit	Kilnamanagh	John Duffy
Gravel pit	Tallaght	John Conlon & brothers
Gravel pit	Corbally	James Kirwan
Gravel pit	Gortlum	Patrick Quinn
Gravel pit	Gortlum	Patrick Quinn
Gravel pit	Aughfarrell	Laurence Nolan
Gravel pit	Ballinascorney upper	John Bagnall
Gravel pit	Friarstown upper	Ponsenby Shaw
Gravel pit	Glassamucky	Maurice Collins (Monk)
Old Gravel pit	Mountseskin	Francis Lynam
Old Gravel pit	Glassamucky	Maurice Collins (Monk)
Sand and gravel pit	Kilnamanagh	Thomas Kealy
Old quarries	Kilnamanagh	John Dodd
Quarry	Belgard	Patrick Cruise
Quarry	Cookstown	Henry Dillon Trant
Quarry	Whitehall	James Delaney

various locations in the parish, including a grouping of quarries at Belgard, Cookstown and Whitehall all adjacent to the present Belgard quarries.

Nine forges were listed in the valuation field books but a number of these were attached to the mills or to the larger farms and may have only served the needs of the farm or mill to which they were attached. This applies particularly to the forges attached to the mill of Michael McDonnell at Oldbawn and the mill of James Sharpe at Templeogue. Otherwise the forge was an important resource in the parish keeping horses shod, manufacturing and repairing various farm implements and making other iron fittings.

The valuation field books also indicate seven public houses in the parish, listed on the next page:

Table 5 Survey of public houses in 1844–5

Townland	Occupier
Tymon North	Nicholas Donovan
Tymon South	James Cullen
Killininney	John McCoy
Tallaght	Peter Dowling
Kiltalown	Michael Clarke
Tymon North	John Cooley
Kilnamanagh	Jane Miley

With some exceptions these can be identified with modern establishments in the area. In particular, the public houses in Tymon South, Killininney, Kiltalown and Tallaght still trade as 'Firhouse Inn', the 'Old Mill', 'Jobstown Inn' and 'The Dragon Inn' respectively. There were three public houses in the area of the Greenhills Road running from Tallaght to Dublin. One of these has survived as the 'Cuckoo's Nest' public house. It is significant that the public houses listed in the townlands of Tymon North, Kilnamanagh, Tallaght and Kiltalown were all located along the main road from Dublin to Carlow that passed through Tallaght with toll gates at Dolphin's Barn, Tallaght and Brittas.[30] This toll road was completed in 1829[31] and still functioned as a toll road in 1854. All tolls were abolished with effect from 5 April 1858 under an 1857 act of parliament, 20,12 Vict., c.16.[32] The other two public houses were at Tymon south and at Killininney, both located on the main road from Dublin or Rathfarnham to Bohernabreena. Thus all of the public houses were located on the two major roads through the parish to serve the needs of travellers as much as local populations.

It seems from the valuation field books that there was only one shop in the parish of Tallaght. This shop was located in the townland of Knocklyon and was occupied by Thomas Browne. Knocklyon townland consisted of 429.75 acres of land with an average valuation of £2.30 per acre making it some of the best quality land in the parish. It was also a very populous townland and located close to Dublin. These circumstances combined to justify a shop in this area at one stage. This shop appeared in the valuation field books in 1844 but the holding was described as a house in the valuation of tenements published in 1850. It appears the shop had ceased to trade in the intervening years. But what of the people of the rest of the parish and where did they source their provisions? Indeed to what extent was there a cash economy in Tallaght at this time? Some commercial ventures in Tallaght served the development of Dublin (the gravel pits) or the needs of travellers passing through the parish (the public houses) and may also have had some local customers. However, it appears from the absence of retail establishments that there was little local demand for shops. There was consistent traffic between the parish of Tallaght and Dublin and in some instances the people of this parish travelled frequently to Dublin both to sell produce and source their provisions. In his letter to Thomas Larcom of 2 August 1837, Eugene O'Curry quotes William Rafter of Glenasmole as saying that the 'Dublin Carmen' alone spoke English in Glenasmole.[33] In the present context this indicates a consistent traffic of carmen between the more remote parts of the parish and Dublin.

Most of the remaining items in the landscape that were revealed in the valuation field books were public institutions such as the court house, police stations, schools and chapels but there were two other commercial entries. The Path Levy House in Templeogue appears to have been located opposite Templeogue House at a point where a laneway led down to a ford for crossing the Dodder River close to Spawell House. This suggests that before the bridges were built at Templeogue and Oldbawn a toll was charged to cross the Dodder by a ford at this point.

Some additional information on economic life in Tallaght is provided by incidental comments in reports of crime during the early 19th century. According to the outrage reports on 23 October 1836 Simon Collins, described as a small farmer from Glassamucky, was assaulted at Firhouse on his way home from Dublin. On 30 November 1836 Patrick McGrath of Kilbride Co. Wicklow (above Ballinascorney Upper) was also assaulted in an attempted robbery at Firhouse while on his way home from Dublin.[34] The reports on several other outrages in the 1830s and 1840s indicate constant traffic between all parts of the parish and Dublin. Other outrage reports indicate a similar traffic between Rathcoole and Saggart and Dublin so that whatever cash was in circulation in the parish may have been spent with businesses and suppliers in Dublin. The outrages were not concerned solely with those small farmers who had the means to travel into Dublin. Several of the reports concern carmen who carried stock to the markets in Dublin and one case illustrates the activities of such carmen. In 1837 Hugh Clarke, a small farmer of Old Mills in Kildare, reported that he was robbed as he passed between Clondalkin and Rathcoole on his way home from Dublin. He had carried pigs into Dublin for a jobber and he had been asked by a family to purchase six loaves of bread and two stone of oatmeal while in Dublin. He was described as a small farmer and was carrying the pigs to Dublin for the 'usual hire'.[35] He was robbed of 6s. 8d., the six loaves and the two stone of oatmeal as he made his way home on his car.[36] Therefore basic provisions were often sourced in Dublin for those areas lying within a short distance of Dublin and families either travelled themselves or hired carmen to purchase their basic provisions for them. Indeed, as the case of Hugh Clarke illustrates, some carmen were nothing more than local small farmers who earned extra income carrying goods, farm produce and provisions to and from Dublin.

There was an established pattern of sourcing basic provisions in Dublin so that whatever cash circulated in Tallaght made its way to Dublin and did not support a local retail economy. This is reflected in Lewis's comment that Tallaght 'has a patent for fairs but they are not held',[37] presumably having been put out of business by the proximity of Tallaght to Dublin. The shop at Knocklyon was for a time an exception to this. This may imply that the demand of those who had risen above the subsistence economy was not sufficiently high to encourage additional shops to open in the parish. The main outlet for those farmers who produced a cash crop appears to have been in Dublin[38] and the necessity for regular travel to Dublin meant that any entrepreneur who would attempt to open a shop in the locality was always in competition with the established Dublin traders. The majority of families who lived in the third grade and fourth grade houses described below (62.4% of families) probably lived at subsistence levels with little or no cash above what was needed to pay rent. This particularly applies to those who had very little land attached to their houses. This cash was earned by labouring on farms or in the mills and these employments were seasonal and intermittent. In some instances rent may have been paid in kind by the provision of labour.

HOUSING QUALITY, ACCOMMODATION AND LIVING STANDARDS

The housing of those who lived in Tallaght is a difficult area to describe. The census returns for 1841 attempted to grade houses and provided figures for the numbers of houses in each parish in each grade. It should be noted that this is an entirely separate system of grading from that adopted by Griffith for his valuation.

The grades used were as follows:

Table 6 Housing grades used in census returns

4th grade	All mud cabins having only one room.
3rd grade	A better description of cottage, still built of mud, but varying from 2 to 4 rooms and windows.
2nd grade	A good farm house, or in the towns, a house in a small street, having from 5 to 9 rooms and windows
1st grade	All houses of a better description than the preceding classes.

Source: *Census, Ireland*, 1841, p. xiv.

Since the census return for 1841 counted and classified houses by parish it is not possible to analyse house grade per townland. However, a useful overview is provided for Tallaght parish and using this with the information provided from Griffith's Valuation below it is possible to arrive at an approximation of house quality per townland. The house grades in Tallaght parish as given in the 1841 census are given in table 7:

Table 7 Housing grades in Tallaght in 1841

Grade	Number of houses (Tallaght)	Number of families (Tallaght)	Percentage of total (Families)	National average %
4th	142	168	19.74	43.5
3rd	326	363	42.66	40.0
2nd	238	273	32.08	15.3
1st	46	47	5.53	1.2
Total	752	851	100	100

Source: *Census, Ireland*, 1841. p. 30.

Fifty houses were reported as uninhabited. The lower grade of housing, one roomed mud cabins, accounted for 18.9% of houses in Tallaght and provided accommodation to 19.7% of families. This compared with a national average for rural families of 43.5% occupying 4th grade housing. Thus the proportion of families in Tallaght living in the poorest grade of housing was less than one half of the proportion living in such housing nationally.[39] While the proportions living in 3rd grade housing was not substantially different from the national average there were higher percentages living in both 2nd grade and 1st grade housing as shown in the above table. This may reflect a number of professional people living on small estates in the parish who derived a living in their professions in Dublin. In the report to this census it was pointed out that in towns and frequently in the country several families resided in the same house.[40] Indeed the same report clarified that an individual either occupying a house, or living as a lodger, but not boarding with the family, was considered to be a distinct family. These comments provide an explanation for the larger number of families than houses in all grades.

The Griffith Valuation field books, which are dated 1844, provide a further insight into housing standards at that time. The grading system adopted by Griffith is outlined in an appendix to the reports relative to the Valuations for Poor Rates and dated 1841.[41] The principal grading system is set out as:

1st   Slated dwelling houses built of stone or brick with lime mortar.
2nd   Thatched houses built of stone or brick with lime mortar.
3rd   Thatched houses having dry stone or mud walls.

New or nearly new houses were classified 'A', medium houses as 'B' and old houses as 'C'.
     Within each of these classes there were subdivisions again as follows:

A+   Built or ornamented with cut stone, and of superior solidity, and finish.
A   Very substantial building, and finish without cut stone ornament.
A–   Ordinary building and finish or either of the above when built 20 or 25 years.

B+   Medium (not new), but in sound order and good repair.
B   Medium, slightly decayed, but in good repair.
B–   Medium, deteriorated by age, and not in perfect repair.

C+   Old but in repair.
C   Old and out of repair.
C–   Old and dilapidated, scarcely habitable.

     Thus a new house, in excellent repair, slated and of superior solidity and finish would be graded 1A+ while an office, a term covering nearly all industrial buildings, built some 20 years previous, with thatching and fair stone walls, might be classed as 2B.
     In terms of relative values the following guidance is given:

> Having ascertained the cubical contents of the house, the valuator next determines to which class it belongs; whether new, medium, or old, and to which division, if any class. If to the first of the new, he will find the price, in proportion to the content, to be five times greater than if it had been the last of the old.[42]

     From this information we can learn a great deal about the quality of housing in Tallaght at the time of the valuation survey in the 1840s. It is also possible to relate some of the information in Griffith's Valuation to the information in the census returns. However, the valuation did not deal with all houses individually. In dealing with houses in the various townlands, the field books almost exclusively described and graded the larger houses. Only those small houses which are listed as gate-houses or which are contiguous to the mills are graded. In other cases the valuation figure allotted to the smaller houses in the surveyors notes in the field books may be used in a comparison with such small houses as are graded to give an approximation of the standard where only the valuation is known. Care must also be exercised when reading this material as houses were measured in rectangular increments for valuation purposes and adjoining offices were included in the same schedules. They can easily be confused.

A study of the valuation field books in relation to house quality reveals that there were 33 large thatched houses in the parish. These were all graded as two or three in the valuation field books. Among these houses was a thatched public house at Tymon South and another at Tymon North. There was a third thatched public house at Kiltalown which had mud walls. There was also a large thatched dwelling in Brittas Big built with mud walls and measuring 58ft long by 18ft wide and another such large thatched house with stone walls at Ballinascorney Lower measuring 77ft in length. The same source indicated there were 107 large slated houses in the parish. Thus the 140 largest houses were described, measured and given a quality grading as set out above in the section of the valuation field books for Tallaght dealing with house quality. No such information was given in relation to the remaining houses in the parish.

Regarding the houses of the poor in the parish a rateable valuation of £2 has been selected below which the housing can be regarded as being particularly basic. There were 412 such housing units in the field books as compiled in 1844. The census for 1841 counted 468 houses as falling into grades 3 or 4 in Tallaght parish[43] and it appears that the study has accounted for 88% of these as having a valuation of under £2. This translates into just 55% of all houses in the parish. For this reason this £2 valuation appears to be a reasonable indicator of the lowest forms of housing. Where such small houses have been graded they were slated, but this information is only available when they were either gate houses or housing provided at the mills. A substantial proportion of the remainder of these small houses were probably thatched. Thus by combining the information in the census returns for 1841 and in the valuation field books compiled in 1844 it is possible to identify and describe the poorest houses in the parish, to count them on a townland basis and to name their inhabitants. There were also a number of thatched farm buildings and stables on some of the farms. This was widespread and it may indicate that on the larger farms with new dwelling houses older dwellings were recycled as stables or other farm buildings.

Many families in the parish lived in very small houses. Sometimes a house may have provided a home to more than one family as can be seen from the numbers of families and of housing units. The information set out in the appendix shows the average household size in the parish between 1841 and 1851. This appendix gathers information from a number of sources and in dealing with 1844 and 1850 information is extrapolated from the valuation field books and from Griffith's Valuation in relation to the population for each of these two years. A list of the townlands of the parish is set out showing the area of each townland, its population for 1841 and 1851 per the census returns, and for 1844 and 1850 as estimated from the number of houses. The number of houses for 1841 and 1851 is taken from the census returns. The numbers of houses for 1844 and 1850 are counted from Griffith's valuation field books and from the Griffith Valuation of Tenements respectively.

Average household size in the parish in 1841 was 6.54 persons and in 1851 it was 6.14 persons per household, taking account of unoccupied houses. If it is assumed that changes in numbers of houses and numbers of people between 1841 and 1844 were not significant then 55% of the dwellings in the parish were rated at less than £2 in Griffith's initial survey in 1844 and by implication a similar percentage of the population of the parish were living in such small houses in 1841. These dwellings were small, typically less than 400 square feet, and 142 of them were mud walled cabins having only one room and no window. The remainder of these small dwellings were in the range of two to four rooms, perhaps with windows. In many cases there was a resident who was not a family member. Houses and offices were measured in ten square foot units and were typically rated at between 1s., and 1s. 8d. per such unit. Thus a small house of medium quality of just 400 square feet would be at the upper limit of the £2 cut off point. To illustrate this, the three gate houses listed in Oldbawn were all rated at less than £2. Two of them were rated at £1 18s. and the third at £1 14s.[44] Five of these houses were rated at less than £1 and by implication they measured something less than 200 square feet.

In the notes describing the larger houses, where a privy or water closet was available it was described and separately rated. It was not present at all the larger houses and there was probably no such facility at the smaller houses. The following houses were all listed as having either a privy or a watercloset during 1844–5 when Tallaght was surveyed:

Table 8 Sanitation facilities in 1844–5

Facility	Townland	Occupier
Privy	Ballymaice	Schoolhouse
Privy	Castlekelly	George Grierson
Watercloset	Templeogue	Charles McDonnel
Privy	Tallaght	Rev. William Robinson
Privy	Ballinascorney Upper	John Bagnall
Privy	Killininney	Charles Devine
Watercloset	Kiltalown	John Robinson
Privy	Oldbawn	John Jordan
Watercloset	Mountseskin	Francis Lynam
Privy	Newlands	Alan Crotty
Privy	Kilnamanagh	John Flanagan

Source: Valuation field books

No other houses were listed as having such a facility at that time and none of the public houses had sanitary facilities. Nor indeed did Dr Burkett, the local dispensary doctor have such a facility at his house. Overall, housing was primitive and basic. In the case of the lowest grade units they were without the facilities of windows and in all cases they were without any type of sanitation. This reinforces the description of housing in the parish given by Dr Burkett in his reply to the Poor Inquiry. He described these cabins as: 'The doors and windows as the only ventilators where the cabin walls are without crack or crevice. Generally deficient of necessary comforts'.[45] A French traveller in Ireland in 1835 described the housing he saw as he travelled from Dublin to Carlow. This road passed through the village of Tallaght and conditions in this parish may have influenced his view: 'Most of the dwellings of the country very poor looking. A large number of them wretched to the last degree. Walls of mud, roofs of thatch, one room. No chimney, smoke goes out the door'.[46] This description matches that of the lowest grade of house in the census return.

Though it was close to Dublin, Tallaght in the first half of the 19th century was a rural place with a local population mostly dependant on agriculture for its existence. The mills, using the Dodder water supply, provided some local employment but not what might be expected so close to the city. The city affected life in the parish in several ways. Firstly, the availability of shops in Dublin and regular travel to the city prevented the development of a local shopkeeper class in Tallaght parish. The various inns and public houses were an exception to this providing relief for travellers on the important roads passing through the parish. Secondly, people with incomes derived from the city maintained a significantly better housing stock in the parish than might otherwise be expected. Thirdly, a wide range of arable crops were grown in the parish for consumption in the city. The city was also supplied with sand and gravel from the parish for its building work. Overall the relationship between Tallaght and its urban hinterland was a complex one and at times an ambiguous one.

2. The people of Tallaght, 1834–44

Two parliamentary reports are crucial to understanding the lives of the people of Tallaght before the Famine. The first is the Poor Inquiry of 1835 and the second was a similar enquiry into the state of education in Ireland. This report was laid before parliament in its 1835 session.[1] The education report enquired into the numbers of persons in communion with the Established Church of Ireland in each parish and also set out to ascertain the number of places of worship belonging to Roman Catholics or Presbyterians and other Protestant dissenters. The number of ministers officiating in each, the proportion of the population of each parish belonging to each persuasion and the numbers attending the services were all inquired into. As its title indicates, this enquiry also gathered information about the means of education in each parish, the numbers and description of schools, the type of instruction offered and the numbers attending. Information on the means of support of each school was also gathered. Seven schools were listed for Tallaght in this report,[2] although Lewis listed eight.[3] These are set out in table 9 overleaf.

There were 283 children enrolled on the books of the daily schools in Tallaght parish in 1834. Some 200 children attended the other schools available. This indicates a school-going population of less than 500 children out of a total population of 4,646 persons in 779 families returned in 1831 in this parish. There are no population figures for 1831 classified by age but the figures for 1841 indicate that 37%[4] of the population of Co. Dublin were classified as being at or under 15 years of age. Using this figure as a measure in 1831 it could be assumed that 37% of 4,646 or 1,719 people were at or under 15 years of age in Tallaght. Thus less than one third of the parish children attended school. This may also suggests that less than one child per family attended school but since more than one child from some families probably attended school it follows that the children of a significant number of families (perhaps in excess of one half of the families of the parish) did not attend any school. The census returns of 1841 indicated that out of the total population of the parish 1,315 people could both read and write, a further 1,018 could read only and 1,919 people could neither read nor write. In that year the total population was returned as 4,921 persons so that 669 people were not accounted for in this literacy analysis. The total number

33

Table 9 Schools in the parish of Tallaght in 1835

Description of each school	Sources of support	Average daily attendance	Kind of instruction
Church male school	The children pay from four shillings to six shillings per quarter	7 or 8	Reading, writing and arithmetic
Church female school	The society for discountenancing vice gives eight pounds a year; the expenses beyond this are provided for by a collection at an annual sermon	June 17; November 14	Reading, writing and arithmetic
Daily school in connection with the national board	Eighteen pounds annually from the national board and payments by the children of one penny or two pence per week.	Winter 108; Summer 144	Reading, writing, arithmetic, and for the females, needlework
School at St Annes monastery	Supported by this religious community who teach the males themselves and pay a mistress for the females.	About 120	Reading, writing, arithmetic and for the females, needlework and straw plaiting
School at the Firhouse nunnery	Supported by the nuns, a few of the scholars being charged one penny a week.	60	Reading, writing, arithmetic and needlework
School kept by James Farrell	Payments by the children of one penny or two pence per week each.	About 51	Reading, writing and arithmetic
Hedge school kept by Margaret Aboyne	The children pay from three pence to five pence per week.	About 12	Reading and sewing

Source: *Public Instruction Inquiry, Ireland*, 1835.

of people returned as having some degree of literacy was 2,333 persons or 47% of the population. Thus significant numbers of people, numbering over one half of the parish population, were illiterate. The infrastructure that conveyed literacy to under one half of the parish is revealed in the Griffith Valuation tables which listed the school premises in the parish at the time of its publication in January 1850 and these are set out in table 10:

Table 10 Schools in the parish of Tallaght in 1850

Townland	Proprietor	Description
Ballymaice	Peter Mahon	National School house and Garden
Tallaght	Elizabeth Deacon	Church Education Society's School house and garden
Tallaght	Jas and Fras McCabe	National School house and garden
Tymon South	Mrs Maginness	Roman Catholic Chapel and School House attached to the Carmelite convent at Firhouse.

Thus seven schools listed in the 1835 survey had become four schools by the end of the 1840s.[5] It is not clear why the number of schools diminished between 1834 and 1850 or whether the numbers attending increased or decreased. The reduction in the population of the parish of Tallaght[6] would not justify a halving of the number of schools. It is clear from the valuation tables that there was an exemption from rates for school houses so that there was no saving in rates for disguising the purpose of a building which was used as a school. It is possible that this represents an amalgamation of schools so the smaller number of schools, particularly the national school, had larger numbers of pupils. The separate church schools for males and females in Tallaght may have amalgamated into the one school under the Church Education Society. The national school referred to above survived, as also did the school attached to the convent at Tymon South. There is no mention of the school kept by James Farrell, the hedge school of Margaret Aboyne, or of the school at St Anne's Monastery. This monastery was located in Glassamucky. The field book reveals that in Glassamucky, Maurice Collins, described as a monk, held three holdings of land including an old gravel pit. Maurice Collins and John Stewart, brothers of the Third Order of Carmelites, founded this monastery and school in 1821.[7] At the date the field books were compiled, June 1845, the buildings on this land were described as including a house, Roman Catholic Chapel, offices, a shed and a Charitable School House. These were all classified as stone buildings with thatched roofs. While a Maurice Collins is listed in the final valuation lists for Glassamucky there is no chapel or school listed at that time. Nor is the word monastery used. This implies that the chapel and school fell into disuse sometime between June 1845 when the area was surveyed, and 1850 when the valuation of tenements was published. However, Handcock[8] describes the hospitality of the monks in 1876 but a footnote to the second edition notes that they had left the place by 1899, so that the monks were there until at least 1876 but appear to have closed the school between 1844 and 1850. The school at Ballymaice cannot be identified with any of the 1835 schools and it seems to have started in the intervening period between 1835 and 1845. In the field book it is graded 1A and this indicates that it was a new building in July 1844 when this area was surveyed.

Tallaght became involved in the national school system in 1832. In that year application was made to the Commissioners for Education for financial aid towards the building and running costs of a new national school.[9] The application is dated 24 September 1832 and the school was established under Mr Thomas Nolan, the master of the boys' school, and Mrs Margaret Nolan, mistress of the girls' school. The school was built at a cost of £200 9s. 4d. and opened for the receipt of scholars on 26 May 1834. The applicants signing the application for National School status were as follows:

James Eager, Tallaght	[Protestant]
John West, Kilnamanagh	[Protestant]
Rev. Fitzpatrick C.C.	[Roman Catholic]
J. Lentaigne, Tallaght House	[Roman Catholic]
Joseph Lentaigne, Tallaght House	[Roman Catholic]
Thomas Donohoe, Brookfield	[Roman Catholic]
Michael McDonnell, Oldbawn	[Roman Catholic]
P.M. Cruise, Belgard	[Roman Catholic]
James McGrane	[Roman Catholic]

Mr J. Lentaigne provided the site for the school and also made himself responsible for the salary of the master and mistress. The application also indicates that Henry D. Trant, who provided materials for the construction of the school from his quarry,[10] was to be appointed a trustee by the board but he did not subsequently appear as a trustee of this school although he was associated with Belgard School. The next applications to the Commissioners for Education in respect of Tallaght are dated 1870 and no schools entered the National System in Tallaght between 1832 and 1870.

PHYSICAL DESCRIPTION OF THE SCHOOLS

The school buildings in which education took place were, in the main, of a good quality and better than most of the other buildings in the parish. In the valuation field book entry for the convent at Tymon South a building is described as a stable and school room and it measured at 50 ft in length by 21 ft in breadth by 17 ft high. It was graded by the quality letter 1C+. In Ballymaice the field book describes 'Belgard School' as measuring 50 ft by 17 ft by 10 ft high. This school was described as new in 1844. There was a privy and store attached and the building was graded by the quality letter 1A. The field book had a note that 'Henry D. Trant Esq. pays a salary to the teacher'. This Mr Trant was a major landlord in the area at the time being the lessor of extensive lands at Allagour, Ballinascorney Upper, Ballinascorney Lower and Ballymaice. Thus with the official institutions of education concentrating at Tallaght and Firhouse (Tymon South) and the closure of the school at Glassamucky, a private benefactor brought a schoolteacher to the uplands at Ballymaice. This is the same Henry Trant who was proposed as, but did not become, a trustee of the new national school at Tallaght. There is less information available on the two schoolhouses in the village of Tallaght. In the valuation field books the first of these, the national school, was located on the Greenhills Road, close to the house of John Lentaigne, the owner of Tallaght Castle at the time. The schoolhouse was described as having 27 perches attached. There is no other information in the field book. But we know from the application made to the Commissioners for Education that this school measured 62 ft by 21 ft with a boys schoolroom, a girls schoolroom and a room for the master. The female school in Tallaght was located close to the Glebe House and was described as a school house and garden. Its grounds extended to 3 roods and 28 perches with an additional area of 2 roods and 10 perches described as waste.

RELIGIOUS PRACTICE

Because of concern about denominational balance in the early 19th century the 1835 public instruction commission was to ascertain the proportion of Protestants and Roman Catholics in each parish in Ireland.[11] The results of the survey in relation to Tallaght are in table 11:

Table II Church attendance in Tallaght in 1835

Denomination	Number of members	Numbers attending Sunday service
Roman Catholic	4214	Friarstown Upper – About 500 Firhouse nunnery – about 150
Established church	326	In Summer, nearly 200 In Winter, 100
Presbyterian	None	n/a
Other dissenters	None	n/a

Source: *Public Instruction Inquiry, Ireland*, 1835.

The survey revealed that 92% of the parishioners of Tallaght were Roman Catholic in 1834. In 1841 this had increased to 93%. Care must be exercised here as the Commissioners' determination of the population in 1841 differed from the census returns for that year and understated the position. From these figures it appears that over one half of the Established Church population attended church. (In summer 1834 54%; winter 27%). Among Roman Catholics Mass attendance was much lower with about 650 attending (15% of the Catholic population). Roman Catholics were served with just two chapels in a very extensive parish. One of these was the nunnery chapel at Firhouse Convent in the townland of Tymon South. The other was located in the townland of Friarstown Upper. There was a third chapel at Glassamucky recorded in 1845 but it is not recorded in the survey in 1834 as providing a place of worship. There was no Roman Catholic chapel in the village of Tallaght itself during the 19th century until the Dominicans took the lease of Mr Lentaigne's House and lands in Tallaght in 1861. They built a monastery and chapel. Thereafter this chapel provided a place of worship for the Roman Catholics in this end of the parish.

The entire diocese of Dublin was listed as having 47 parish priests and 106 curates or assistant priests in 1834. No parish priest was listed for Tallaght but Fr Roche was listed as parish priest of Rathfarnham, Bohernabreena and Crumlin at that time. He had two curates, Fr Fitzpatrick and Fr Brennan. The problems of attending in the various chapels of this extensive area to say Mass every Sunday could have been demanding but priests lived adjacent to each of the chapels at Rathfarnham, Crumlin and Friarstown so that each had a local responsibility. The inquiry reported that one Mass was said in Friarstown Upper each Sunday and two were said in the nunnery chapel. The entry in the 1834 return for the nunnery chapel at Tymon South (Firhouse) stated that the chaplain of that society officiated there. One Mass at each chapel each Sunday was the norm in most of

Ireland at the time.[12] Whether for this reason or for some others, attendance at Mass was low. Travel for priests and parishioners was difficult. Those not in possession of a horse had to walk everywhere and in this parish there were substantial distances to cover, sometimes in upland terrain.

The townlands of Tymon South, Knocklyon and Killinniney could be regarded as the population out of which attendance at Firhouse Convent Chapel was drawn. The population of this area in 1841 was 490. On the basis of the 1834 return just 30% of the population reasonably contiguous to the chapel were actually attending Mass in this chapel. The situation at the chapel at Friarstown Upper was not very different. This chapel was located at the site of the present chapel adjacent to Friarstown House. The chapel was an L shaped structure measuring 2,000 square feet. The overall height was measured at 12 ft. Average attendance here was reported as being 500 people. It seems that the adjacent townlands including the valley of Glenasmole had a population of 1,518 people in 1841. Therefore about one third of this population attended Roman Catholic Mass regularly at Friarstown Upper. It may also be that some of the population from Kingswood, Newlands Demesne, Belgard, Cookstown, Kilnamanagh and Tallaght Village itself attended Mass in Clondalkin. Similarly people in the north-eastern end of the parish may have gone to Rathfarnham parish church with whom they shared their parish priest and curates. Some of those from the townlands of Kilnamanagh and Tymon North may have gone to Crumlin parish church. However Clondalkin parish at this time had a population of 3,086 Roman Catholics and regular attendance at church service of 900 people. This was a higher incidence of Mass going than in Tallaght parish and may reflect an easier physical landscape. In Clondalkin also, out of a total Church of Ireland population of 327 there were 80 churchgoers in winter and 100 in summer. The results of the survey indicated that Mass attendance in the area of South Dublin/Wicklow averaged 20–40% of the Catholic population in 1834.[13] The pattern of Mass attendance in Tallaght in 1834 was at the lower end of what was typical at the time and for the region. The Public Instruction Inquiry of 1834 also reported that the population of Established Church members was declining because of emigration at the time.

IRISH LANGUAGE

Part of the process of making the Ordnance Survey maps of the 1830s was collecting information about the area being mapped. The surveyors talked to local people about folklore and customs in the course of ascertaining local place names for their maps. Many of these discussions were recorded in their

letters to Thomas Larcom, who supervised the survey from Mountjoy
Barracks in the Phoenix Park.[14] In his letter to Larcom dated 2 August 1837,
Eugene O'Curry, an Irish scholar, described his conversation with William
Rafter of Castlekelly, in Glenasmole. Rafter was 84 years old at that stage
and O'Curry described his Irish as being as 'good Irish as ever I heard
spoken, as does his sister Una'. O'Curry reported being told by Rafter that
40 years previously very few spoke English in this glen. He also said that
very few men over 40 didn't understand Irish and didn't speak it. It also
seems from O'Curry's account of the incident that William Rafter was
exceptional in being able to speak fluent Irish in Glenasmole in 1837. It
appears that Irish was spoken up to 40 years before that but died out after
that date. The Dublin carmen were described as the exceptions, having no
knowledge of Irish[15] and we may conclude that influence from Dublin city
was one reason why English replaced Irish as the spoken language in the
glen during that 40 year period.

THE POOR OF TALLAGHT, 1834–44

In 1835 the Poor Inquiry (Ireland) was laid before parliament. Its aims were
set out in the introduction with the words: 'To determine what measures
might be requisite to ameliorate the condition of the poorer classes in
Ireland, required an investigation extending to almost the whole social and
productive system; for the poorer classes in Ireland may be considered as
comprehending nearly the whole population'.

The commissioners therefore determined that the inquiry should
embrace every subject to which importance seemed to have been attached
by any large number of persons.[16] The Poor Inquiry carried out a detailed
survey in one parish in each barony in selected counties. Unfortunately this
detailed enquiry did not include a barony in Co. Dublin. However, the
enquiry was conducted in the nearby parishes of Castledermot, Kilcock,
Naas, Osberstown, and Rathangan in Co. Kildare.

In addition to this detailed survey more general questionnaires were
issued to all other parishes in the country. The first questionnaire dealt with
the relief of the destitute classes in Ireland. In relation to Tallaght Revd
Laurence Roche P.P. answered this questionnaire[17]. The Poor Inquiry sought
information under seven general headings and these are set out in table 12:

Table 12　The scope of the Poor Inquiry

Deserted and orphan children

Illegitimate children and their mothers

Widows having families of young children

The impotent through age or other permanent infirmity

The sick poor, who in health, are capable of earning their subsistence

The able bodied out of work

Vagrancy as a mode of relief

Source: *Poor Inquiry (Ireland): First report from Her Majesty's Commissioners for inquiring into the condition of the poorer classes in Ireland*, 1835 (369), vol. xxxii, appendix A, p. v.

The questionnaire circulated was not always answered by a clergyman and the quality of the answers given varied greatly around the country. One gentleman in the parish of Kilcroan, Co. Galway answered almost every question 'I am not informed upon the object of this enquiry.'[18] On the other hand many respondents answered much more comprehensively than the Catholic priest, Revd Roche did in Tallaght. It appears that Revd Roche, together with two curates, administered the parishes of Rathfarnham, Crumlin and Tallaght.[19] It further appears that one of the curates, Revd Fitzpatrick, was based in Bohernabreena and would have had more detailed knowledge of the area of Tallaght.

DESERTED CHILDREN IN TALLAGHT

One of the problems highlighted by the Poor Inquiry was that of deserted children, which it tried to quantify. The area for which Revd Laurence Roche provided answers to the commissioners questions extended from Crumlin to Cruagh, including both Tallaght and Bohernabreena and was totally rural in 1835. This area, combining three parishes, was reported to have a population of 13,098 people. He reported one deserted child in the area who died. Even though the answers given by Revd Roche were short they indicated that at least one deserted child existed in the area under his jurisdiction and there were probably more in so large a population. By contrast the same report set out the responses of Revd J. Hayden, Church of Ireland vicar in the nearby parish of Rathcoole with a population of 495 people.[20] He reported three deserted children. This man also gave much more detailed replies to the other questions and it must have been easier to be in touch with the problems of the substantially smaller parish. The minutes of the Select Vestry in Tallaght for 2 July 1833 recorded that Ben Bradley and Patrick Mathews were appointed overseers for deserted children in the parish[21] indicating that this problem needed a structured response.

The report of the enquiry held at Naas, to the south of Tallaght parish, set out some more detailed information.[22] In Naas, it was reported that there were about 5 current deserted children and about 50 orphans; there was an annual average of about 8 deserted children. The opinion was expressed in Naas that the number of deserted children had increased during the last five years and that deserted children 'are always illegitimate and occasionally perish before they are discovered'.[23] In Naas, deserted children were cared for by being put out to nurse to women in the parish and a sum of £5 per year was granted for their support. The Naas Enquiry also heard that there was no hospital for deserted children since the closing of the Foundling Hospital in Dublin. This inquiry was also told that orphans received no support because the law made no provision for them. For the Tallaght–Bohernabreena–Crumlin area Revd Roche reported that there was not one bastard child who was without the support of either father or mother. Whatever number of bastard children was in the area Revd Roche contended that they were not deserted. His report differed from the Naas report, which reported numbers of deserted children and where one of those attending the public hearing, Mr Goodwin Esq., stated that deserted children were always illegitimate. The report by Revd Roche dealt with an extensive area of which Tallaght was only part. Though the population of Naas Parish and Tallaght Parish was almost identical it must be considered that Naas was a larger town and was the county town. It was also an important coach stop with strong links into a wider world. Tallaght, by contrast, was a rural district with a population of just 348 people in the village out of a total parish population of 4,921 people in 1841. Revd Roche's report was dealing with a large combined area containing almost three times the population of Naas and this area was located close to the city of Dublin. The incidence of deserted children thus differed in different areas.

Appendix C of the Poor Enquiry reported that in Dublin during the years 1831, 1832, 1833 and 1834 there were 49 cases of desertion with 27 of these found alive and 22 found dead; there were just 7 inquests.[24] The same report set out that in Kildare for the same period there were 86 cases of desertion with 78 of these found alive, 8 found dead and just 6 inquests. Deserted children appear to have been a greater problem in Kildare than in Dublin and this evidence corroborated that of Revd Roche. In summary it seems that what bastard children there were in Tallaght were well supported by either their fathers or mothers and that there was very little desertion of children. But the problem necessitated the appointment of overseers for deserted children by the Select Vestry. Revd Roche reported that one child was abandoned at a farmhouse and subsequently died. If the practice in Naas was followed then at least some of those found alive would have been put to nurse. The position of orphaned children was at least as drastic with poor families unable to make provision for them and no official form of relief available.

Tallaght Parish had another role in relation to Dublin's deserted children. The Poor Inquiry report[25] set out details of charitable education in Dublin. Two Roman Catholic associations within the city of Dublin, The Virgo Mariah and the Cholera Orphans' Association reported that they placed destitute orphan children in their care with small farmers in Bohernabreena and Tallaght for rearing until eligible for apprenticeship at from 11 to 15 years of age. Preference was given to dairy farmers when selecting foster homes for these children. In return foster families received a fee, and the report set out that the annual cost of each orphan was six guineas. In this way people in Tallaght parish were playing a role in helping to deal with Dublin's destitute orphans.

THE ELDERLY AND INFIRM

As well as the children the other main groups that the Poor Inquiry identified as receiving social support were the elderly and the infirm. The remaining questions in the Inquiry's questionnaire dealt with these groups. Revd Roche answered that he did not know exactly how many people there were in the parish who from old age or infirmity were incapable of work. He thought that many were in great want and were supported by charity but had no example of this. In this case also we can look at Naas.[26] Two answers were given in the replies to the questionnaire. One respondent replied that there were about 50 such elderly people who supported themselves exclusively by subscriptions and begging. Another respondent thought that 80 to 100 such infirm elderly supported themselves by begging. If this state of affairs was transferred to Tallaght then there may have been in the range of 50 to 100 old and infirm people in the parish who resorted to begging to support themselves. It can be calculated from the 1841 census figures that approximately 10.6% of the 1841 population of rural Dublin were aged 51 or over.[27] By extension there were approximately 522 people in this age group in Tallaght at the time. The 1841 census also sets out that average life expectancy was 38.5 years for a 5-year-old male and 40 years for a five-year-old female.[28] Those over 51 years were exceptionally old making up just 10% of the population. An estimation that between 50 and 100 old and infirm people in Tallaght had to resort to begging to live accounts for 10% to 20% of the total population in this age range and seems reasonable.

The Poor Inquiry reveals the limited support that the elderly and infirm received. In Naas there was no fund available to give aid to the poor when sickness brought destitution on them.[29] Their only assistance was from neighbours and cholera was the only sickness that prevented the poor from attending to one another, so great was the horror of it. Where gruel was provided it was useless because they had no way of heating it in this precarious world. At Naas it was the opinion of all present that the wages of a labourer would not enable him to lay by any provision against a time of sickness; nor even could a small farmer do so, after paying rent and supporting his family. At Kilcock it was also reported that 'a short illness is often ruin to the labourer.'[30] In these circumstances for a labouring man to fall ill meant inevitable destitution unless there were neighbours or relatives to support the family.

MIGRATION AND BEGGING

Migration was a characteristic feature of local society in Ireland before the Famine. Some of those were emigrating and the Church of Ireland population of Tallaght was described as declining through emigration in the Public Instruction survey. However, most migration was local in nature. Revd Roche reported that very few labourers left the parish of Tallaght to obtain employment in England.[31] This may indicate that there was sufficient, if erratic, work available in the immediate area or in Dublin but such a situation would set Tallaght apart from its neighbouring parishes. In Naas, for instance, it was reported that, generally, married men who were labourers locked up their homes and put their wives and children out to beg while they were away for seasonal work.[32] It was further reported from Naas that 'those who go from this parish to England in search of work, amount to about 40 or 50 yearly; they do not beg their way, Dublin being so near.'[33] At this time the Revd Hayden of Rathcoole observed that 'five or six men go to Fingal to cut down meadows or reap corn on lands near Dublin, wherever the crops ripen sooner than in this parish. I never knew a labourer to have gone to England from this parish.'[34] In contrast to Naas, Revd Hayden reported that the wives left behind in Rathcoole subsisted by the 'previous leavings or the produce of a little crop; all of them have cabins'.[35] There were more mixed replies from nearby Clondalkin, Lucan and Palmerstown in the same report.[36] It appears that many men from these areas got employment during the building season in either Dublin or Liverpool. As at Naas though, the wives and children strolled about in search of relief while the men were away.[37]

It seems that Tallaght and Rathcoole had a different pattern of migration to that of Naas. In Tallaght the report stated that very few left the parish to go to England. From Rathcoole there was migration within the greater

Dublin area but nobody went to England. From Naas, 40 to 50 left for England each year, virtually abandoning their families to do so. While this is a small sample it seems to indicate that those closer to Dublin had extra employment opportunities available to them and therefore less need to adopt the drastic measure of leaving their families to migrate to England.

An explanation for the lack of migration from Tallaght may be the employment opportunities provided by the several mills located along the Dodder in the townlands of Oldbawn, Tallaght and Templeogue. Such opportunities would have provided some income to provision families and pay rent in these townlands. Thus the need for labouring men to migrate in search of work may not have been so great as around Naas. Revd Roche was answering for a much larger district than the parish of Tallaght and both Rathfarnham and Crumlin were located closer to the city of Dublin. His reply may have been influenced by conditions in those areas where people could work in Dublin but he may also have been correct in relation to Tallaght because of the employment available in that area.

Many of the migrants recorded in the Poor Inquiry were regarded as beggars. When asked about beggars in Tallaght Revd Roche answered simply 'cannot tell.'[38] However, he thought that about 80 houses in the area of his combined parishes let lodgings for strolling beggars at 2*d*. or 3*d*. per night. The census summary for 1841 returned 81 persons over the age of 15 years deriving their living from providing lodgings in the parish of Tallaght.[39] This reflected high demand for such facilities, partly the result of the proximity to Dublin and was a source of cash for households. The evidence from neighbouring areas gave a clearer image of the phenomenon of beggars and strolling beggars. In respect of the neighbouring parish of Rathcoole Revd Hayden answered, 'there are dry lodging cabins, who will accommodate every character, beggar or not, who will pay; the common fare is 3*d*. per night for a feather bed and 2*d*. for a chaff ditto.'[40] He reported about six indigenous beggars in his area with a total population of 495 persons. This represented just over 1% of his population. Both replies in respect of Kilcullen[41] reported 38 beggars out of a population of 2,918 or 1.3% of that population.

In many of the parishes in the Tallaght area it was reported that several or many people gave lodgings to strolling beggars. The charge levied varied from free to 2*d*. or 3*d*. per night. For instance Wm. Henry Carter Esq in Kilcullen with a population of 2,918 reported that about 120 households gave such lodging. The report for Lucan may give one reason for so much mobility. Here the answer was given that 'the numbers of beggars varies exceedingly. When any new public work is spoken of about Dublin, multitudes travel up long distances in hopes of being employed'.[42] It appears that the villages on the approaches to Dublin had many beggars passing through in search of whatever work was rumoured to be available.

The problem of vagrancy was clearly significant. At Naas it was reported that the number of vagrants in that parish amounted to about 250, and had been increasing substantially.[43] It was creating a nuisance to shopkeepers and the coach offices. As the county town and as a main stop on the coach routes Naas may have had a larger number of beggars than other places. Some of the beggars in that locality could be successful, collecting up to three stone of potatoes per day, an amount that a Mr Lalor described as certainly more than he could consume. The same Mr Lalor also described that the 'go between, bouthy, or matchmaker, would collect double that quantity, their business being to carry messages from the farmers' daughters to their bachelors, and to look out for husbands for them.'[44] Thus some few of the beggars made their travelling a lucrative occupation. Much of the deliberation of the Naas Inquiry was concerned with the causes of vagrancy and with ensuring that any relief schemes adopted did not have the effect of encouraging vagrancy. It was also observed at Naas by one of the labourers who attended that it was 'the farmers and shopkeepers who were more open to the calls of beggars ... the relief of that class falls chiefly on them. The rich have their gatekeepers, and the beggars dare not go past them. Even the labourers, who have but their hire to depend upon, give part of their meals and a night's lodging to the beggars.'[45]

As already pointed out Tallaght had a similar population to Naas and had a number of houses willing to provide lodgings. It was also positioned on a main road to Dublin from west Wicklow and Carlow, including the Carlow Turnpike and was close to the road from Cork to Dublin. It thus had its share of vagrants. Revd Roche's comment that he could not tell how many persons in the parish subsisted by begging does not suggest that there were none or few in this category; merely that he did not know how many. The experience of other localities suggests that there may have been as many as 50 beggars in the Tallaght area.

THE DISPENSARY

R.P. Burkitt, Esq. M.D. was the local dispensary doctor at Tallaght in the 1830s dealing with a much smaller area than that reported on by Revd Roche, as he was the dispensary doctor to Tallaght, Ornagh (now known as Orlagh) and Saggart. Dr Burkitt had to visit and treat the sick poor in their homes and attended one dispensary every day. He attended all cases personally where medical or surgical aid was required. He reported that his annual 'case load' varied from 1,000 to 1,200 cases per year over the period from 1831 to 1833.[46]

Dr Burkett's salary was 100 guineas or £105 per annum but if he allowed his expenses, including cost of medicines and rent, to become excessive he suffered a reduction in his annual salary sufficient to balance the books. He received his full salary in 1833 only out of the three years covered by the inquiry. For this amount of money and an additional £22 worth of medicine the dispensary service provided relief to 1,000 or 1,200 persons per annum. According to the 1831 census Tallaght had a population of 4,646 persons and Saggart another 1,671. Ornagh was part of the parish of Cruagh and had 20 persons.[47] Therefore the total population for which Tallaght dispensary was responsible was 6,337 persons. Approximately one sixth of this population was availing of the dispensary service. Industrial accidents in the mills were clearly a problem and there was an outbreak of cholera in the area in 1832 and one of influenza in the year 1834.

Dr Burkitt also discussed the nature and causes of diseases and he considered want of proper food as a most important cause of disease and iterated that a rule of diet is an important feature of treatment. He described people as 'generally badly clad and eating food of a coarse sort, sometimes deficient in quantity, and not suited to whatever diseases the people suffer from'. Their bedding was described as consisting of a blanket and bad quilt and a coat or cloak thrown on straw often upon the ground. He also described badly furnished and ventilated cabins, 'which are deficient of the necessary comforts'. His reference to the doors and chimney being the only source of ventilation indicated that many of the cabins of the poor were without windows. Since the doctor made a point of describing it as one of his duties to attend at the homes of his patients when required and to be in daily attendance at the dispensary[48] he was therefore in a position to know the daily lives of the poorest in the parish in a way that Revd Roche could not.

The Griffith Valuation schedules and field books indicate that Dr Burkitt had his residence in the townland of Oldbawn both in 1844 and in 1850,[49] close to many of the 'manufactories' mentioned in his report. The valuation field book reveals that his house was classified as 'Ia' and measured 42ft by 19ft and stood 10.5ft tall. It had a projection measuring 14ft by 8ft and a return of 16ft by 13.5ft. It had a shed attached and a basement underneath. Outside were to be found an office, cow house, stables and store. There may have been a loft over one of the sheds for the storage of fodder. His house and yard stood on just over 21 acres of what was described as 'good gravelly and deep loamy arable land and was adjacent to part of the river strand. From the valuation map for the area it appears that his house was located close to Oldbawn Bridge on the north-east side of the Oldbawn Road. It was originally named 'Mountain View' and subsequently became known as 'Bawn Villa'. The grading 'Ia' indicated that his house was slated and built of stone or brick with lime mortar. It was new or nearly new and a very substantial building finished without cut stone ornament. This house was still occupied up to approximately 1970.

No detailed information was gathered by the Poor Inquiry concerning the dispensary at Tallaght other than the questionnaire referred to above. However, the inquiry did conduct public examinations at a number of other dispensaries and the results of these examinations give a basis for describing the issues with which Robert Burkitt MD and his various subscribers were concerned. Many of the dispensary reports in the Dublin area mentioned vaccination against smallpox. This was still relatively new having been developed by Dr Jenner in 1796.[50] At Baldoyle in north Co. Dublin there had been frequent cases of the disease in more recent years and it was reported that the medical officer thought that the confidence of the public was a little shaken. At Clane and Donadea in north Kildare the opposite was reported. Here vaccination was performed every day when applied for and smallpox was not recently common in the area. 'The confidence of the public in the efficacy of the vaccination appears from the numbers that are vaccinated to be increasing.'[51] At Celbridge, close to Tallaght, the medical officer reported that 'he considers vaccination to be decidedly preventive of smallpox, which has very seldom appeared in the district of late years. The confidence of the public is gradually increasing in its efficacy'.[52]

Access to dispensary services was clearly a difficult issue as was funding them. At Baldoyle the medical officer reported that nobody was ever refused advice or medicine but that to have a recommendation from a subscriber was the regular course for accessing the services available. 'Many of the farmers and some others who subscribed required that they themselves, their families and all living on their farms should be attended gratis'.[53] This seems to echo the answer of Dr Burkitt to the Poor Inquiry when he wrote of the holders of small portions of land who were recommended by subscribers as proper objects. At Clane the report stated that a recommendation from a governor entitled a person to relief. 'The servants of subscribers are attended'. Here also it was reported that 'neither is attendance given gratuitously to any of the poorest subscribers'. This contrasted with the position reported in Baldoyle. The Celbridge report sets out the rule in that area.

> Those who have obtained the recommendation of a subscriber are alone entitled to relief. Each subscriber is, however permitted to issue an unlimited number of orders, so that no person can, under ordinary circumstances, be excluded from the benefits of the institution, which there is no reason to believe are extended to any others than those whose circumstances place them really in need of gratuitous assistance. The lower servants of subscribers are considered to come within the latter description, but neither advice nor medicine is ever given to a subscriber as such.[54]

The subscribers of a minimum of one guinea each elected a governing committee of not less than five people and the county, through the grand jury, was authorised to match the annual subscription.[55] Concern was expressed in some of the reports that the dispensary committee could arrange subscriptions so as to persuade the county to pay a higher amount.[56] This seems to imply that some of the 'subscriptions' were made in return for some consideration. These were the politics behind the answer by Dr Burkitt to the question concerning persons receiving the assistance of the dispensary though not strictly entitled to it. In their report the Poor Inquiry commissioners set out some general introductory facts and at page 15 of this introduction they made a comment about 'Houses of Industry',[57] as workhouses were sometimes called, which bears repeating for its summation of attitude:

> Wherever we met with these institutions, they appeared to be a real blessing to the community. Some of them, we thought, might be improved in principle; some we considered to have found the exact limit of relief, beyond which allowances to the poor ought not to pass, and indeed cannot pass, without acting as an encouragement to idleness and improvidence; some were just touching upon that dangerous boundary. Upon the whole, however they deserve the very warmest encouragement of the legislature.[58]

The dispensaries appear to have had a pharmacy in which were stored quinine and morphia among other drugs. Clane, Donadea and Celbridge reported that leeches were available when symptoms rendered them expedient. We can safely assume that at Tallaght Dr Burkitt kept a supply of quinine and morphia among his medicines and that he also used leeches to bleed patients when considered efficacious. He would also have been expected to vaccinate against smallpox but public acceptance of vaccination and public confidence in its effectiveness varied depending on local experience and perception. There would have been midwives in the locality but the doctor may have become involved in difficult cases.[59] The dispensaries investigated did not have any great supply of surgical instruments and at Celbridge these were confined to those used in the extraction of teeth. Apart from these instruments the medical officer was obliged to have recourse to his own stock of instruments.[60] At Clane the dispensary reported that they possessed splinters, bandages etc to render assistance in case of fractures or other injuries. Mention was also made that no extra payment was made to the medical officer for the use of his horse, which he had to supply from the salary provided.

PUBLIC ORDER

The all pervading poverty of the time predisposed some of the inhabitants of
Tallaght to crime. There was a petty sessions court in Tallaght and in
Rathfarnham and their work gives some idea of the normal business of the
criminal and tortuous litigation in the district.[61] Fines were imposed in large
numbers of cases for trespass, for assaults and for the 'illegal manufacture or
sale of spirituous liquors'. Cases of trespass on growing crops were among
those dealt with and such disputes occurred in Upper Glenasmole.[62]
Rathfarnham also dealt with about 100 cases taken for the recovery of wages
over the three years from 1831 to 1833 and it was reported that £122 6s. 2d.
was claimed and £59 5s. 9d. was awarded. Rathfarnham also reported that
no claims were made in that court for the maintenance of bastards and that
if they had, they would have been referred to the parochial churchwardens.
Celbridge Petty Sessions court took a different approach where those who
should have supported bastards were summoned for wages due for nursing
and the claims were disposed of as claims for wages due. This court also
reported that fines collected for illegal manufacture of spirituous liquors
were sometimes used to pay the informers. Some evidence of more serious
crime is contained in the minutes of the Tallaght Select vestry. In 1826 in
addition to applotting the county cess the following two claims for
compensation were applotted locally: burning, £11 7s. 6d. and maiming
cattle, £40. In May 1834 in addition to the county cess an amount of £92
10s. was applotted for malicious burnings. In 1851 in addition to the county
charge a sum of £19 19s. was levied on the townlands of Allagour and
Ballinascorney Upper and Lower for malicious injury.[63]

The Outrage Papers also set out details of the more serious crimes in the
parish between 1836 and 1850.[64] In the years 1836 to 1839 27 outrages were
reported for the civil parish of Tallaght. The crimes dealt with were varied
and included a theft of arms, several cases of 'firing at the person',
threatening letters, and many cases of sheep, horse and cattle stealing. In both
1836 and 1839 some of the crimes reported arose out of evictions. Four of
the seven reported outrages in 1836 were connected to one eviction, which
took place in Glassamucky in March of that year. Similarly in 1839, three of
the nine reported outrages concerned one family in Kiltalown and their
eviction.

The Poor Inquiry and the Public Instruction Inquiry set out set out basic
information in relation to the lives of the people who lived out their lives in
Tallaght. Basic education was available to those who could afford it in a
selection of schools made available through charity or through the support
of parents. A minority of the children of the parish could avail of this
education. A school under the new national system came to Tallaght in 1832

and functioned side by side with schools made available by religious orders and by local landlord support. Attendance at church services and at Mass was low reflecting a difficult landscape and limited availability of Mass.

The lives of the poor, a majority of the local population, were miserable. People were not paid sufficient to save anything towards illness or towards the support of orphaned children. When illness struck there inevitably followed utter destitution and homelessness. Patterns of migration among the population of Tallaght were different in that the local people did not resort to emigration but were able to get some work locally or in Dublin. Tallaght had its share of travelling beggars and these people generally migrated in search of seasonal work, begging as they travelled, and staying overnight with those families who provided the most basic lodgings.

A dispensary service was available providing basic medical attention to the poorest of the parishioners. Dr Burkett provided this service and he has left us some intimate comments on the lives of the poorest in Tallaght. It is small wonder that these poor sometimes found themselves falling foul of the law. The courts dealt with ordinary civil matters such as trespass and actions for wages due. But cases of assault, illegal distilling and petty theft also came before the courts regularly. Tallaght also had some incidence of more serious crimes arising out of agrarian troubles and evictions indicating the dependence of many local people on access to land to survive.

3. Changing trends, 1841–51

The appendix charts the changes in population in each townland in the parish of Tallaght during the crucial Famine decade from 1841 to 1851. The year 1841 is the first year for which population statistics are available by townland. Over that period the population of the parish of Tallaght fell from 4,921 people in 1841 to 4,367 people in 1851 representing a fall of 554 persons or 11.3% of the 1841 population. Nationally the population fell by 20.3% of the 1841 figure in the same period. Thus the rate of decline in population in Tallaght during the Famine decade was just over one half of the national average decline for that period. However the timing and extent of this population decline was by no means constant over the whole parish but varied from townland to townland depending on the type and quality of land occupied, the involvement of the landlord in estate management and on local employment opportunities.

Using a £1 per acre valuation as a mid point the parish can be divided into poor land (less than £1 per acre) or better land (greater than £1 per acre). In the case of the poorer land the population fell to 82% of its 1841 level by 1851 and further declined to 71% by 1871. This compares with a decline to 93% and 77% respectively from the better land. This is illustrated in table 13.

Table 13 Comparison of decline from poorer and better land

Year	Index of decline from poorer land	Index of decline from better land
1841	100	100
1851	82	93
1861	73	79
1871	71	77

The fall in population was clearly substantially less from the areas of better quality land than from the poorer land in the period as a whole. In particular the fall in population was substantially less from the better land in the years before 1851.[1]

The appendix also sets out an analysis of population in relation to household size and house numbers for 1841, 1844, 1850 and 1851. House numbers are taken from the respective census returns for 1841 and 1851 and have been counted from the valuators field books for 1844 and from the Valuation of Tenements for 1850. The Valuation of Tenements for Tallaght was issued in January 1850 and reflects the position in late 1849. The effects of the Famine can be more closely examined using these sources rather than depending on the 1841 and 1851 census figures alone. According to the census average household size was 6.54 individuals per occupied house in 1841 and this had fallen to 6.14 individuals per occupied house in 1851. There was an increase in occupied houses in 1844 over 1841 of one additional occupied house. This implies an increase of six or seven people in the population of the parish in those three years, if we assume no change in average household size. In order to assess the population in 1850 we have assumed a constant rate of decline in average household size from 1844 to 1851. This gives an average household size of 6.20 persons per occupied house in 1850. These households occupied 695 houses indicating a lower population of 4,307 persons in that year with a recovery in house numbers to 711 houses occupied by 4,367 people in 1851. This indicates that Tallaght suffered an immediate population decline during the Famine with some rapid recovery from this decline by 1851. Thereafter there was a continuing decline in population concurrent with the national decline.

But within this generality there are anomalies which require further attention. The townland of Oldbawn, for instance, saw a growth in population from 302 people in 1841 to 382 people in 1851. This was exceptional among rural townlands at the time and it may be related to improved employment prospects in the mills at the Dodder. By 1861 the population of this townland had fallen back to 339 persons, a decline from the 1851 level but still larger than the population in 1841. In 1871 it had declined further to 235 persons. Another anomaly is provided by Ballycullen which had a population of 19 people in 1841 and 21 people in 1851 and yet had only one dwelling house. This was a substantial house and the occupier was listed as Peter McGrath. This individual occupied about 250 acres in the townlands of Ballycullen, Ballycragh and Tymon South. No house was listed in Ballycragh. Only one large house was listed in Ballycullen. There were two houses listed for Tymon South associated with Peter McGrath. A farm of that size required a substantial labour supply in 1841. It appears that this farmer may have housed his labourers in Tymon South. Mr McGrath may have had a very large family at Ballycullen which subsequently left the area. By 1861 the population of Ballycullen had fallen to 4 people.

OLDBAWN AND GORTLUM IN THE PERIOD 1841–51

In understanding population change, the townlands of Oldbawn and Gortlum provide contrasting case studies. The field books indicate that Oldbawn was a heavily industrialized area with several mills working in 1844. It is distinguished by the fact that its population rose during the period from 1841 to 1851 in contrast to the totality of the parish. By contrast Gortlum had no industry and was an upland farming area whose experience of the Famine decade may be expected to be more typical of the country as a whole.

Comparing the houses and occupiers as recorded for Oldbawn in the Griffith Valuation with the valuation field books of 1844 reveals where changes in population happened. There were 50 occupied houses in this townland according to the 1841 census return[2] and 54 occupied houses were listed in the valuation field books, which were surveyed in 1844. There was an increase of only four occupied houses over the number returned in the 1841 census implying a population increase of 26 persons. Then 50 occupied houses were listed in the valuation of tenements list published in 1850.

The 1851 census return counted 66 occupied houses in the townland. This was a substantial increase of 16 occupied houses in the ten year period for 80 additional people and this increase happened between the issuing of the valuation of tenements in January 1850 and the census in 1851. There were twelve occupiers listed in Griffith's Valuation (1850) who were not listed in the field books (1844). Most of these were adjacent to McDonnell's Paper Mills while 11 others listed in 1844 were no longer there in 1850. Most of these changes reflect substantial turnover of tenants, and perhaps of staff at McDonnell's mill. This substantial increase in the population of Oldbawn at the very end of the decade, when considered together with the earlier evidence of expansion of the buildings at McDonnell's paper mill indicates that the employment lately available at this mill drew a new population to the townland of Oldbawn.

In Gortlum the population was 112 people with 14 occupied houses in 1841. By 1851 the population had fallen to 59 people in nine occupied houses. Nine occupied houses were also recorded in Griffith's Valuation lists in 1850. The field books were surveyed in July 1844 and counted 10 occupied houses. They included two names and two houses which had disappeared by 1850. The two names are Michael Gibney and Alice Donagh. In the case of Gibney, this man had no land and the note in the field book beside his name read 'now widow Tyrrel' followed by 'broke down'. There is a line drawn through the valuation for the house. There was no area of land involved with this house but it seems to have been located in Patrick Quinn's holding. Alice Donagh's house also disappeared and her holding seems to have merged with that of Terence Healy. It seems that the two disappearances noted resulted from consolidation of the holdings of Quinn and Healy during the period from 1844 to 1850. The first four holdings listed in the valuation did not change from the listing in the field books. In the case of Quinn, his holding was listed under two separate lot numbers in the field book. It was a similar case with Healy whose valuation listing consisted of three separate holdings in the field book. There was no change to McDonagh's holding. The Hodgens holdings were shown separately in the field book but listed as a joint holding in the valuation list. Daly's house remained unchanged, as did that of Murray and Brady. There is some evidence of Quinn and Healy having consolidated their holdings and it may be that this was the end of a process of consolidation that may have started before the 1841 census and had almost finished by the time of the valuation survey in 1844. It can be seen from the appendix that occupied house numbers fell from 14 in 1841 to ten in 1844 and that population fell from 112 to 80 in the same period. Population further declined to 61 people in 1850 and 59 people in 1851. The number of occupied houses reduced to nine in 1850 and remained at nine in 1851. The population reduction in this townland substantially happened by 1844 and was not a result of the Famine.

The Famine did not have the same effect everywhere. While the overall effect in Ireland was of a 20% population reduction the Famine was also a catalyst for change. The population increase which had happened prior to that decade forced people to occupy marginal land and these people were poorest and suffered most. This is demonstrated in Tallaght by the greater reduction in population on this poorer land during the Famine decade. But the pressure for change was also an opportunity for those in a position to benefit. A landlord at Gortlum resisted the pressure for further subdivision on his land and started a process of consolidation of holdings before 1844. His tenants improved their farms and their families remained in that location well into the twentieth century. At Oldbawn there was a decline in population during the Famine but a mill owner was in a position by the end of the decade to expand his enterprise and increase employment thus initiating a substantial increase in population close to his mill.

Conclusion

Tallaght parish had some amelioration from the general condition of poverty in Ireland in the years 1835 to 1850. The Poor Inquiry of 1835 examined poverty under a number of headings which are set out in the introduction to the report. The responses of those with direct knowledge of the parish and accounts of the public inquiries in neighbouring areas reveal that except for quality of housing the degree of poverty in South Dublin/ North Kildare was extreme. Tallaght may have differed from places further from Dublin in that there was little evidence of migration from Tallaght to England in particular in search of seasonal work. There was such evidence in relation to Naas to the south of Tallaght. The report from Rathcoole, west of Tallaght indicated migration, particularly of farm labourers, within the greater Dublin area. It seems that migration to England was a feature of life in areas further removed from Dublin.

In the case of deserted and illegitimate children in Tallaght it was contended that whereas such children existed they were never deserted and it was indicated that the farmers of the Tallaght/Bohernabreena area were providing a nursing service to two homes for deserted children in Dublin. The existence of two overseers for deserted children appointed by the Select Vestry in Tallaght also evidences an established structure for such children in the parish. In the case of the elderly or infirm they frequently resorted to begging to survive. It can be estimated that c. 50 to 100 such people lived by begging in the Tallaght area at any one time. Beggars and strolling beggars were a feature of the pre-Famine landscape and these abounded in both Tallaght and elsewhere. Many were men in the process of migrating for work and those with long journeys to the ports begged their way to Dublin, or other ports, as part of the journey to England for seasonal work. Many of these passed through Tallaght and it is probable that houses in Tallaght provided lodgings for them. Revd Roche, the Catholic priest, had no knowledge of these migrants and other beggars but inquiries in other parishes close to Tallaght revealed the extent of vagrancy. The Poor Inquiry was preoccupied with the problem of vagrancy to the extent that almost one half of the local inquiry reports were given over to consideration of this one aspect of poverty. Illness was also a disastrous event in the lives of the poor and the sources indicate that the wages earned by the labouring poor did not enable them to provide for a period when they could not earn. It appeared that the dispensary doctor was conscious of this and recommended that a proper arrangement be made to supply the poor with wholesome food.

The dispensary provided a free health service to those certified by a subscriber to be eligible. There was also a requirement that the dispensary doctor visit the poor in their homes when circumstances so required. His reports gave an intimate account of the poor. He particularly reported on poor quality diet and on very poor housing conditions in the area. From the other dispensary reports it was seen that smallpox vaccination was being promoted but that not everybody was confident of its efficacy. The politics of the dispensary service were such that sometimes those not entitled to its services could avail of them because of the influence of the subscribers and the dispensary doctor was concerned about this.

The housing conditions provide another indicator of relative poverty. The grading system adopted for the census of 1841 indicates that there were 142 of the poorest 4th grade of houses in Tallaght housing 168 families. These were spread out over the whole parish with clusters of them adjacent to several of the mills. However the proportion of families living in 4th grade housing in Tallaght was less than one half of the proportion of families living in such accommodation nationally and there were proportionally more people living in 1st grade and 2nd grade housing. Despite the evidence of the Poor Inquiry housing conditions indicate that poverty in Tallaght was not so widespread or pervasive as in other rural areas. But the dispensary doctor's description indicated that the poorest in Tallaght were living in very poor one room cabins with no ventilation, little or no furniture nor proper bedding.

Church going was not a priority among members of either major religious group in the area. However, it appeared that the incidence of Mass attendance among Roman Catholics was slightly lower than was typical for the region at that time. D.W. Miller's survey found Mass attendance at between 20% and 40% for this region in 1834 whereas for the parish of Tallaght it averaged 15%. While the Roman Catholic population of the parish grew, some reduction in the established church population was remarked on and attributed to emigration. There were seven schools listed in the parish in 1834 and this had reduced to four schools in 1850. These schools catered for less than one third of the population under 15 years of age and the incidence of illiteracy was high. The census of 1841 indicated that an estimated 53% of the people of this parish were illiterate.

Part of the explanation for the fact that Tallaght was not so poverty stricken as other parts of Ireland may lie in the limited industrial activity in the area offering alternative employment. There were several mills in the area powered from the Dodder River. These mills provided extensive employment locally. It appears from the reports on working conditions that both paper and cloth mills were suffering from competition from the improving technology of the English mills and several of the reports on combinations refer to the problems being caused by this competition. Conditions appear to have been worsening for mill workers and declining levels of wages in the woollen industry were reported. The workers at the mills at Haarlem in Oldbawn were the object of a charitable trust and some were perceived to be destitute. Other mills were located in the townland of Tallaght and in Templeogue and a total of 123 families were chiefly employed in manufacture or trade. Despite its closeness to Dublin and the availability of waterpower Tallaght had average levels of industrial employment and slightly higher levels of agricultural employment than the national average at the time.

Again the industrial base may help to explain the unusual impact of the Famine in Tallaght. There was an overall population reduction, which was more severe from the townlands with poorer land quality. But the overall reduction was 11.26% compared to a national population reduction of 20.3% in the same period. Thus Tallaght did not suffer to the same extent as other parts of Ireland. From the summary and comparison of house quality it appears that Tallaght was more prosperous and better housed than the average for the rest of Ireland in 1841. It also appears that there was an expansion of employment opportunities in Oldbawn associated with the paper mill at about 1850. As seen in Gortlum there was evidence of consolidation of land holdings and a reduction in its population at an early stage in the period.

There was also a reduction in house numbers in the parish from 802 to 775 between 1841 and 1851 and an increase in unoccupied houses from 44 in 1841 to 63 in 1851 which suggests emigration as whole households move away. The increase in employment and population in Oldbawn appears to have happened at the very end of the decade because there was no significant increase in house numbers from the 1841 census to the valuation of tenements published in 1850. This indicates that the increase in house numbers and by implication, in population happened at the very end of the decade. In Gortlum it appears the substantial decrease in population in this area had already happened by 1844 when the surveyors' field books were prepared. Other evidence in the field books indicates that a process of consolidation of holdings was nearing completion here in 1844 as the valuation survey was underway.

In looking at the changes in the Famine decade it is important to look closely at the factors influencing change in each townland to determine whether the effects of the Famine are to be used in explaining change or whether other influences were being wrought. The available sources have facilitated such an examination in relation to Oldbawn and Gortlum. This indicates the period during the decade when the population changes happened in each townland. It is only where the changes coincide with the three years of the Famine that we can conclude they were caused by it. Otherwise other factors independent of that calamity were causing change during this unhappy decade.

Conditions in Tallaght and the changes which happened there were influenced by its situation close to Dublin. In spite of this closeness the parish remained rural in character. The availability of shops and markets in Dublin retarded the development of such facilities in Tallaght. Public houses catering for travellers, gravel pits supplying the construction industry and forges serving the local population were the main small enterprises in the area. The various mills on the Dodder provided industrial employment but only to such an extent that agriculture remained the source of employment for over 76% of families in the parish. Tallaght had higher dependence on agriculture and lower dependence on industrial employment than much of the rest of Ireland at the time. Many of these farmers grew a crop or milked cows supplying their output to Dublin and in this way Dublin had positive influence on agricultural viability in the area. These factors reinforced the rural character of the parish. The existence of numbers of good houses on small portions of land indicates people with sources of income in Dublin paying for the upkeep of such houses. This, together with the relative prosperity of farming, contributed to the parish having better than average housing quality at the time. From these origins has emerged the present Tallaght, a major national centre for industry and services, shopping and healthcare and with a past that had a very different experience of these central aspects of its people's lives.

Appendix

Summary of population movement in Tallaght 1841–51

Townland	Area Acres	1841 Occupied houses	Population
		1841	
Aughfarrell	581.75	13	99
Allagour	83	9	65
Ballinascorney lower	177.25	9	62
Ballinascorney Upper	2275.75	41	260
Ballycragh	102.5	1	2
Ballycullen	112.25	1	19
Ballymaice	170.75	11	78
Ballymana	444.5	14	79
Ballymorefinn	532.25	16	126
ballyroan	114.25	5	38
Belgard	323	10	55
Belgard Deerpark	124	0	0
Bohernabreena	231.75	2	18
Brittas Big	140.25	3	20
Brittas Little	250.75	6	48
Castlekelly	2797.25	14	84
Cookstown	264.5	2	9
Corbally	523.75	11	72
Corrageen	21.75	4	28
Cunard	257.25	10	58
Friarstown Lower	54	5	38
Friarstown Upper	179.25	9	65
Garranstown or Kingswood	122.75	3	20
Gibbons	247.75	7	56
Glassamucky	422	23	147
Glassamucky Brakes	1115.5	16	96
Glassamucky Mountain	176	0	0
Glassavullaun	1090.5	12	79
Gortlum	342.25	14	112
Jobstown	420.5	8	65
Killinarden	515.25	20	148
Killininny	194.5	11	61
Kilnamanagh	621.5	24	153
Kiltalown	277.25	14	92
Kiltipper	193	5	33
Knocklyon	429.75	45	305
Lugmore	122.5	6	49
Mountpelier	919.75	34	219
Mountseskin	715.75	7	47
Newlands Demesne	70.25	3	13
Oldbawn	615.25	50	302
Oldcourt	436	7	61
Piperstown	381	14	95
Tallaght	1052.5	24	142
Templeogue	671.25	76	479
Tymon North	483.5	25	137
Tymon South	105.25	15	124
Whitehall	122.75	2	30
Whitestown	241	7	62
Tallaght town		57	348
Greenhills town		27	123
Total	**21867**	**752**	**4921**
Average household size (persons)			**6.54**

60

1844		1850		1851	
Occupied houses	Population	Occupied houses	Population	Occupied houses	Population
13	99	13	76	11	61
6	43	5	37	5	37
8	55	8	51	8	50
47	298	45	252	42	230
0	0	0	0	0	0
1	19	1	21	1	21
10	71	10	77	9	70
12	68	11	55	9	44
16	126	16	119	13	96
2	15	2	11	3	15
7	39	5	33	5	34
0	0	0	0	0	0
2	18	2	8	2	6
3	20	2	12	3	18
6	48	6	46	5	38
15	90	12	76	11	70
4	18	5	26	5	27
9	59	11	73	12	80
4	28	4	21	3	15
9	52	9	60	9	61
9	68	9	64	9	63
5	36	6	32	5	25
5	33	5	32	4	25
7	56	6	42	6	41
23	147	21	151	16	117
15	90	14	85	14	85
0	0	0	0	0	0
12	79	12	87	10	74
10	80	9	61	9	59
8	65	8	58	7	50
22	163	20	140	21	146
9	50	9	48	10	53
44	281	45	291	23	149
12	79	10	67	11	74
4	26	4	30	4	31
50	339	42	244	46	259
5	41	5	38	5	37
35	225	22	142	27	175
9	60	7	33	8	35
1	4	2	5	1	2
54	326	50	291	66	382
8	70	6	48	7	55
14	95	13	96	13	97
108	640	50	286	38	217
77	486	64	383	70	416
17	93	22	98	27	115
9	74	10	58	13	69
2	30	2	14	3	16
5	44	5	40	5	39
0	0	50	289	55	375
0	0	0	0	22	113
753	4946	695	4307	711	4367
	6.57		6.20		6.14

Notes

INTRODUCTION

1 Richard Griffith, *Tenement valuation of Ireland* (Dublin, 1850), p. 74 (hereinafter cited as Griffith's Valuation 1850).

2 The list of townland names in this map in figure 2 is taken from Griffith's Valuation 1850. The topography is described from Ordnance Survey map sheet 50 in the Discovery Series.

1. THE PHYSICAL WORLD OF TALLAGHT, 1835–44

1 Ordnance Survey of Ireland. Discovery Series, sheet 50.

2 Samuel Lewis, *A history and topography of Dublin city and county* (Cork, 1980), p. 234.

3 Griffith's Valuation, 1850, Valuators field books. Parish of Tallaght.

4 Griffith's valuation, 1850, six inch valuation Map.

5 W.A. McCutcheon, 'The use of documentary source material in the Northern Ireland survey of industrial archaeology', in *Economic History Review*, 19 (1966), 401.

6 John D'Alton Esq., *The history of the county of Dublin,* (Dublin, 1838), p. 757.

7 Griffith's Valuation, 1850, Valuators field books, parish of Tallaght.

8 H.G. Leask, 'House at Oldbawn' in *Journal of the Royal Society of Antiquaries of Ireland*, 43 (1913), 314.

9 *Poor Inquiry, Ireland, First report from her Majesty's Commissioners for inquiring into the condition of the poorer classes in Ireland, HC 1835 (369)*, XXXII (Hereinafter cited as *Poor Inquiry, Ireland, 1835)*, appendix C, p. 523.

10 Wm Domville Handcock, *History and antiquities of Tallaght* (rpr. Cork, 1976), p. 59.

11 Valuation Office, Valuation Field Books Co. Dublin.

12 *Poor Inquiry, Ireland*, 1835, appendix C, pp 535–7.

13 Ibid.

14 Ibid.

15 D'Alton, *The history of the County of Dublin*, p. 757.

16 McCutcheon 'Industrial archaeology', p. 404.

17 Domville Handcock, *History and antiquities of Tallaght,* p. 129.

18 McCutcheon., 'Industrial Archaeology', p. 404.

19 Domville Handcock, *History and antiquities of Tallaght*, p. 137.

20 Michael Herity (ed.), *Ordnance Survey letters: Dublin* (2001) p. 35.

21 R. Refausse and M. Clark (eds), *A catalogue of the maps of the estates of the archbishops of Dublin 1654–1850* (Dublin, 2000), plate 22.

22 Description taken from the Valuation field Books.

23 V. Jackson, 'Inception of the Dodder water supply', in *Dublin Historical Journal*, 15:2, (1959), 33.

24 Valuation field books for County Dublin. Valuation Office.

25 *Census, Ireland,* 1841.

26 Patrick Lynch and John Vaizey. *Guinness's Brewery in the Irish economy* (Cambridge, 1960), p. 168.

27 *Census, Ireland,* 1851, p. 223.

28 *Census, Ireland,* 1851, p. 223.

29 Constantina Maxwell, *Dublin under the Georges, 1714–1830* (Dublin, 1946), ch. 2.

30 David Broderick, *The first toll roads* (Cork, 2002), p. 209.

31 Ibid., p. 266.

32 Ibid., p. 272.

33 Herity (ed.), *Ordnance Survey Letters: Dublin*, p. 22.

34 Outrage Papers, Dublin, 1836, Box 34, National Archives of Ireland.

35 Outrage Papers Dublin, 1837, Box 27, National Archives of Ireland.
36 A horse-drawn cart.
37 Lewis, *History and topography*, p. 234.
38 *Thoms Directory*, 1850, and *Shaws Directory*, 1850, indicate a well developed market for agricultural produce in Smithfield, Spitalfields and in the area around Arran Street. There were also some farm implement makers both in Smithfield and Arran Street.
39 *Census, Ireland*, 1841. p. xvii.
40 *Census, Ireland*, 1841, p. xvi.
41 *Appendix to reports relative to the valuation for poor rates, Ireland 1841.* Supplement, p. 828.
42 Ibid.
43 *Census, Ireland*, 1841. p. 30.
44 Map reference 4b, 4l and 9b in valuation of tenements.
45 *Poor Inquiry, Ireland*, 1835, supplement to appendix B, p. 187.
46 Emmet Larkin (ed. & trans.), *Alexis de Tocqueville's Journey in Ireland, July–August 1835* (Dublin 1990), p. 39.

2. THE PEOPLE OF TALLAGHT

1 *Public Instruction inquiry, Ireland*, 1835.
2 *Public Instruction inquiry, Ireland*, 1835. Second Report, p. 517.
3 Lewis, *History and topography*, p. 234.
4 *Census Ireland*, 1841.
5 In Tallaght some of the check valuations were carried out by the valuators in 1848 and finalised thereafter. The final Valuation of Tenements list was published in January 1850. This was about 15 years after the Public Instruction Inquiry was conducted in 1834. See field books (201).
6 See the appendix setting out population figures per townland for the years 1841 to 1851 and taken from the various census returns.
7 Patrick Healy, 'The valley of Glenasmole' in *Dublin Historical Record* (August 1961), 119–20.
8 Wm Domville Handcock, *History and antiquities of Tallaght*, p. 77.
9 Initial application to the Commissioners of Education at ED1/28. National Archives of Ireland.
10 Lewis, *History and topography*, p. 236.
11 D.W. Miller, 'Mass attendance in Ireland in 1834', in Steward Brown and David Miller (eds), *Piety and power in Ireland, 1760–1960: essays in honour of Emmet Larkin* (Notre Dame, 2000), pp 158–79.
12 Ibid. at table 7.1
13 Miller, 'Mass attendance in Ireland in 1834', p. 173.
14 Herity (ed.) *Ordnance survey letters: Dublin* (Dublin 2001), p. ix.
15 Ibid. p. 22.
16 *Poor Inquiry, Ireland*, 1835, first report, p. 7.
17 *Poor Inquiry, Ireland*, 1835, appendix A, p. 873.
18 *Poor Inquiry, Ireland*, 1835, appendix A, p. 813.
19 *Public Instruction Inquiry, Ireland*, 1835, appendix II.
20 *Poor Inquiry, Ireland*, 1835, appendix A, p. 875.
21 Minutes of Select Vestry of Tallaght. Representative Church Body Library, Dublin.
22 *Poor Inquiry, Ireland*, 1835, appendix A, p. 27
23 *Poor Inquiry, Ireland*, 1835, appendix A, p. 28.
24 *Poor Inquiry, Ireland*, 1835, appendix C, p. 583.
25 *Poor Inquiry, Ireland*, 1835, appendix C, p. 477.
26 *Poor Inquiry, Ireland*, 1835, appendix A, p. 577.
27 *Census, Ireland*, 1841, general tables. p. 33.
28 *Census, Ireland*, 1841, appendix to the report. p. lxxxii.
29 *Poor Inquiry, Ireland*, 1835, appendix A, p. 319.
30 *Poor Inquiry, Ireland*, 1835, appendix A, p. 319.
31 *Poor Inquiry, Ireland*, 1835, appendix A, p. 873.
32 *Poor Inquiry, Ireland*, 1835, appendix A, p. 877.
33 *Poor Inquiry, Ireland*, 1835, appendix A, p. 573.

34 *Poor Inquiry, Ireland,* 1835, appendix A, p. 875.
35 *Poor Inquiry, Ireland,* 1835, appendix A, p. 875.
36 *Poor Inquiry, Ireland,* 1835, appendix A, p. 871.
37 *Poor Inquiry, Ireland,* 1835, appendix A, p. 871.
38 *Poor Inquiry, Ireland,* 1835, appendix A, p. 873.
39 *Census Ireland,* 1841, appendix, p.31.
40 *Poor Inquiry, Ireland,* 1835, appendix A, p. 875.
41 *Poor Inquiry, Ireland,* 1835, appendix A, p. 877.
42 *Poor Inquiry, Ireland,* 1835, appendix A, p. 871.
43 *Poor Inquiry, Ireland,* 1835, appendix A, p. 573.
44 *Poor Inquiry, Ireland,* 1835, appendix A, p. 573.
45 Ibid.
46 *Poor Inquiry, Ireland,* 1835, appendix B, p. 547.
47 *Census Ireland,* 1831.
48 *Poor Inquiry, Ireland,* 1835, appendix B, p. 723.
49 Valuation field books. Also; Griffith's valuation of Tenements, 1850.
50 J.O. Thorne and T.C. Collocott (eds), *Chambers biographical dictionary* (Edinburgh, 1984), p. 731.
51 *Poor Inquiry, Ireland,* 1835, appendix B, p. 123.
52 *Poor Inquiry, Ireland,* 1835, appendix B, p. 343.
53 *Poor Inquiry, Ireland,* 1835, appendix B, p. 121.
54 *Poor Inquiry, Ireland,* 1835, appendix B, p. 342.

55 *Poor Inquiry, Ireland,* 1835, appendix B, p. 31.
56 *Poor Inquiry, Ireland,* 1835, appendix B, p. 123.
57 O'Connor, John, *The workhouses of Ireland* (Dublin 1995), p. 31.
58 *Poor Inquiry, Ireland,* 1835, appendix B, p. 15.
59 *Poor Inquiry, Ireland,* 1835, appendix B, p. 125.
60 *Poor Inquiry, Ireland,* 1835, appendix B, p. 342.
61 *Poor Inquiry, Ireland,* 1835, supplement to appendices D, E &F, p. 371.
62 William Nolan, 'Society and settlement in the valley of Glenasmole *c.*1750–*c.*1900', in F.H.A. Aalen and Kevin Whelan (eds), *Dublin city and county from prehistory to present* (Dublin, 1992), p. 181.
63 All recorded in Minute Book of the Select Vestry in Tallaght. RCB Library.
64 Outrage Papers, Co. Dublin. National Archives of Ireland.

3. CHANGING TRENDS, 1841–51

1   The census return for 1871 contains a note to the effect that Greenhills did not then contain a sufficient number of houses to constitute it a town. The population has therefore been included in that of the townlands of Kilnamanagh and Tymon North. Both these townlands of good land show an increase in population in 1871 over that in 1861. Care should be exercised in drawing conclusions in relation to 1871.
2   *Census, Ireland,* 1851, p. 42.